Nocturnal revels: or, the history of King's-Place, and other modern nunneries.with the portraits of the most celebrated demireps and courtezans of this period The second edition, corrected and improved, with a variety of additions. Volume 2 of 2

Monk of the Order of St. Francis

Nocturnal revels: or, the history of King's-Place, and other modern nunneries. ... with the portraits of the most celebrated demireps and courtezans of this period: ... By a monk of the Order of St. Francis. In two volumes. ... The second edition, corrected and improved, with a variety of additions. Volume 2 of 2

Monk of the Order of St. Francis

ESTCID: T115739

Reproduction from British Library

Vol. 1 has the edition statement on both its titlepage and half-title; vol. 2 has the edition statement only on its half-title. "Order of St. Francis", the burlesque order established by Sir F. Dashwood at Medmenham Priory.

London : printed for M. Goadby, 1779.

2v. ; 12°

Eighteenth Century
Collections Online
Print Editions

Gale ECCO Print Editions

Relive history with *Eighteenth Century Collections Online*, now available in print for the independent historian and collector. This series includes the most significant English-language and foreign-language works printed in Great Britain during the eighteenth century, and is organized in seven different subject areas including literature and language; medicine, science, and technology; and religion and philosophy. The collection also includes thousands of important works from the Americas.

The eighteenth century has been called "The Age of Enlightenment." It was a period of rapid advance in print culture and publishing, in world exploration, and in the rapid growth of science and technology – all of which had a profound impact on the political and cultural landscape. At the end of the century the American Revolution, French Revolution and Industrial Revolution, perhaps three of the most significant events in modern history, set in motion developments that eventually dominated world political, economic, and social life.

In a groundbreaking effort, Gale initiated a revolution of its own: digitization of epic proportions to preserve these invaluable works in the largest online archive of its kind. Contributions from major world libraries constitute over 175,000 original printed works. Scanned images of the actual pages, rather than transcriptions, recreate the works *as they first appeared.*

Now for the first time, these high-quality digital scans of original works are available via print-on-demand, making them readily accessible to libraries, students, independent scholars, and readers of all ages.

For our initial release we have created seven robust collections to form one the world's most comprehensive catalogs of 18th century works.

Initial Gale ECCO Print Editions collections include:

History and Geography
Rich in titles on English life and social history, this collection spans the world as it was known to eighteenth-century historians and explorers. Titles include a wealth of travel accounts and diaries, histories of nations from throughout the world, and maps and charts of a world that was still being discovered. Students of the War of American Independence will find fascinating accounts from the British side of conflict.

Social Science

Delve into what it was like to live during the eighteenth century by reading the first-hand accounts of everyday people, including city dwellers and farmers, businessmen and bankers, artisans and merchants, artists and their patrons, politicians and their constituents. Original texts make the American, French, and Industrial revolutions vividly contemporary.

Medicine, Science and Technology

Medical theory and practice of the 1700s developed rapidly, as is evidenced by the extensive collection, which includes descriptions of diseases, their conditions, and treatments. Books on science and technology, agriculture, military technology, natural philosophy, even cookbooks, are all contained here.

Literature and Language

Western literary study flows out of eighteenth-century works by Alexander Pope, Daniel Defoe, Henry Fielding, Frances Burney, Denis Diderot, Johann Gottfried Herder, Johann Wolfgang von Goethe, and others. Experience the birth of the modern novel, or compare the development of language using dictionaries and grammar discourses.

Religion and Philosophy

The Age of Enlightenment profoundly enriched religious and philosophical understanding and continues to influence present-day thinking. Works collected here include masterpieces by David Hume, Immanuel Kant, and Jean-Jacques Rousseau, as well as religious sermons and moral debates on the issues of the day, such as the slave trade. The Age of Reason saw conflict between Protestantism and Catholicism transformed into one between faith and logic -- a debate that continues in the twenty-first century.

Law and Reference

This collection reveals the history of English common law and Empire law in a vastly changing world of British expansion. Dominating the legal field is the *Commentaries of the Law of England* by Sir William Blackstone, which first appeared in 1765. Reference works such as almanacs and catalogues continue to educate us by revealing the day-to-day workings of society.

Fine Arts

The eighteenth-century fascination with Greek and Roman antiquity followed the systematic excavation of the ruins at Pompeii and Herculaneum in southern Italy; and after 1750 a neoclassical style dominated all artistic fields. The titles here trace developments in mostly English-language works on painting, sculpture, architecture, music, theater, and other disciplines. Instructional works on musical instruments, catalogs of art objects, comic operas, and more are also included.

The BiblioLife Network

This project was made possible in part by the BiblioLife Network (BLN), a project aimed at addressing some of the huge challenges facing book preservationists around the world. The BLN includes libraries, library networks, archives, subject matter experts, online communities and library service providers. We believe every book ever published should be available as a high-quality print reproduction; printed on-demand anywhere in the world. This insures the ongoing accessibility of the content and helps generate sustainable revenue for the libraries and organizations that work to preserve these important materials.

The following book is in the "public domain" and represents an authentic reproduction of the text as printed by the original publisher. While we have attempted to accurately maintain the integrity of the original work, there are sometimes problems with the original work or the micro-film from which the books were digitized. This can result in minor errors in reproduction. Possible imperfections include missing and blurred pages, poor pictures, markings and other reproduction issues beyond our control. Because this work is culturally important, we have made it available as part of our commitment to protecting, preserving, and promoting the world's literature.

GUIDE TO FOLD-OUTS MAPS and OVERSIZED IMAGES

The book you are reading was digitized from microfilm captured over the past thirty to forty years. Years after the creation of the original microfilm, the book was converted to digital files and made available in an online database.

In an online database, page images do not need to conform to the size restrictions found in a printed book. When converting these images back into a printed bound book, the page sizes are standardized in ways that maintain the detail of the original. For large images, such as fold-out maps, the original page image is split into two or more pages

Guidelines used to determine how to split the page image follows:

• Some images are split vertically; large images require vertical and horizontal splits.
• For horizontal splits, the content is split left to right.
• For vertical splits, the content is split from top to bottom.
• For both vertical and horizontal splits, the image is processed from top left to bottom right.

NOCTURNAL REVELS:
OR, THE
HISTORY
OF
KING's-PLACE,
AND OTHER
MODERN NUNNERIES.

CONTAINING THEIR
MYSTERIES, DEVOTIONS, and SACRIFICES.
Comprising also, The
ANCIENT and PRESENT STATE of PROMISCUOUS GALLANTRY.

WITH THE
PORTRAITS of the moſt CELEBRATED DEMIREPS and COURTEZANS of this PERIOD:

AS WELL AS
Sketches of their Profeſſional and Occaſional Admirers.

By a MONK of the ORDER of St. FRANCIS.

VOL. II.

Il vero eſt, quod ego mihi puto palmarium,
Me reperiſſe, quo modo adoleſcentulus
Meretricum ingenia & mores poſſit noſcere:
Mature ut cum cognorit, perpetuo oderit.
TER. EUN. Act 5. Sc. 4.

LONDON.
Printed for M. GOADBY, Pater-noster-Row.
1779.

NOCTURNAL REVELS:

OR, THE

HISTORY

OF

KING's-PLACE,

AND OTHER

MODERN NUNNERIES.

SECOND EDITION.

VOL. II.

NOCTURNAL REVELS:

OR, THE

HISTORY

OF

MODERN NUNNERIES.

CHAP. XXIII.

Reflections upon the Utility and Advantage of Public Stews. Some Account of Foreign Prostitutes. The Policy of conniving at Female Prostitution. An historical Sketch of the Treatment, Honours and Homage of the Courtezans of Athens, with some Remarks upon the same.

HAVING thus far pursued our plan, with a few illustrative digressions by way of Episode; the Rea-

der

der may, perhaps, be inquisitive to know, especially if he should chance to be a Methodist, whether we are the advocates for Vice or Virtue? Indeed the question is curious, if not pertinent, and worthy of being adverted to. The present state of Gallantry and Intrigue being now exhibited, let us for a moment consider what advantages and evils may result from it. In most polished countries, the Police judiciously wink at peccadillos of this kind. In the reign of Elizabeth, we had licensed stews, in various parts of the Metropolis and suburbs. In France, which is universally allowed to be one of the most refined Kingdoms in the World, the Serails (or Seraglios, as we have already mentioned them) are not only countenanced, but even protected. In the capital cities of Holland, particular districts are allotted for the residence of Courtezans, out of which

which stations they must not appear. At Venice they are tolerated, on condition of wearing stockings of two different colours. In fine, Female Prostitution has been considered by all wise legislators as a necessary evil, in order to preclude a greater, which may easily be suggested; and the reason is obvious. Men, in various situations of life, are so circumstanced, that it would be very imprudent to enter into the marriage-state: Family-alliances may have destined them for a particular match, not yet ripe for being entered upon: Indigence may point out to them the various difficulties that will naturally arise from a connubial alliance: No female object may, as yet, have sufficiently attracted their attention, to create a permanent or solid passion, sufficient to erect so important and indissoluble a structure as that of

marriage:

marriage: In fine, from a variety of caufes, circumftances, and contingencies, it may be very ineligible for many men to enter into the ftate of wedlock; and yet they may be animated with, and actuated by, the moft violent amorous paffions. Nay, even in the ftate of matrimony itfelf, it often happens, that a man who holds his wife in the higheft eftimation, may be debarred the felicity of hymeneal raptures, from ficknefs, abfence, and a variety of other temporary caufes, which may with facility be imagined. If, in any of thofe fituations, a man could not find a temporary relief in the arms of Proftitution, the peace of Society would be far more difturbed than it is. The brutal Ravifher would ftalk at large, and might plead, as in the cafe of hunger, that the violence of his paffion would break down even ftone walls:

No

No man's wife, sifter, or daughter would be in a state of security: The rape of the Sabines would be daily rehearsed, and anarchy and confusion ensue. In this point of view then, at least, female proftitution should be winked at, if not protected; and though it may be pronounced a moral evil, it certainly is a political good.

LET us for a moment take a retrospect of the opinion of that sagacious people the Athenians, upon this subject. The Courtezans figured here with great eclat; and it may gratify the curiosity of the Reader to enquire, by what means this order of women, who at once debased their own sex, and in a great measure disgufted ours, in a country where the women in general were distinguished by their rigid morals, ob-

tained

tained efteem, and often the higheft pinnacle of celebrity. Various reafons
may, upon enquiry, be affigned. Firft,
Courtezans were to a great degree
blended with religious ceremonies. The
Goddefs of Beauty, who had altars confecrated to her fhrine, was confidered as
their Patronefs, and whom the Athenians
worfhipped. They invoked Venus in
times of the greateft peril. The uncommon fame of Miltiades and The-
mistocles was in a great meafure owing to the Lais's finging hymns to the
Goddefs after their battles, and thereby
confecrating their victories. The Courtezans were alfo connected with Religion, through the cultivation of the arts.
They offered themfelves for models to
copy Venus's, who were afterwards adored in their temples. Phrynia ferved as
a model to Praxiteles for the Venus
which

which gained him fo much renown, and during the feafts of Neptune at Eleufis, Apelles having feen this fame Courtezan run along the banks of the river, without any other covering than her flowing treffes, was fo ftruck with her beauty, that from her he took his idea of Venus rifing from the flood.

Thus were they of infinite utility to Painters and Sculptors, to whom they furnifhed ideas of the moft tranfcendant beauty, and tended greatly to embellifh their works. They were, moreover, great muficians, as well vocal as inftrumental The art of mufic, which was of the highett eftimation in Greece, communicated additional charms to their perfonal and mental qualifications.

The enthufiafm of the Athenians for beauty was fo great, that their vivid

ima-

imaginations inebriated them even to idolatry in their temples, which were decorated with the masterly productions of the artist. It was the chief object of contemplation in their games and exercises Premiums were allotted it, in their public festivals; and it was even the ultimate end of their matrimonial rites. But it should be observed, that with regard to the immaculate part of the sex, solitary beauty was necessarily obscured, and concealed from the general eye; whilst the charms of Courtezans assailed every spectator, and compelled general homage.

THE intercourse of Society can alone develope the captivating charms of the mind all other females were excluded from this privilege The Courtezans living publicly in Athens, incessantly and

and involuntarily heard Philofophical
Difquifitions, Political Debates, and
Poetical Flights; and as it were im-
perceptibly caught a tafte for learning
It neceffarily followed, that their mental
faculties were improved, and of courfe
their converfation became more brilliant.
Hence it was, that their houfes became
academies of claffical paftime:—Poets
reforted hither in fearch of the Mufes, as
well as the Graces, and Satire frequently attended with truly Attic farcafm, to
give a *gufto* to the literary repaft Even
profeffed Philofophers did not think it
beneath their rigid dignity to attend.
SOCRATES and PIRICLES often met at
the houfe of ASPASIA, fomewhat fimi-
lar to St. EVREMOND's frequently vifiting the celebrated NINON DE L'ENCLOS.
That delicacy of expreffion, that refinement of tafte, which can only be caught
from the Fair-Sex, was here feized with

avidity. In return, the reputation of a *Demirep* received a borrowed luftre from fuch diftinguifhed guefts.

GREECE was governed by men of elocution, profeffed orators, and rhetoricians; and Courtezans having it in their power to gain an afcendency over the greateft Logicians, confequently had confiderable influence in the government of the State. DEMOSTHENES, the terror even of tyrants, was compelled to fubmit to the impulfe of their charms, to the tyranny of beauty; and it was faid of him, with equal truth and poignancy, " That the ftudy of years " was annihilated in an hour's conver- " fation with a fine woman."

PHRYNIA had a golden ftatue erected to her memory, at *Delphos*, between the Maufoleums of two Kings; and the

death

death of many Courtezans was succeeded by magnificent monuments, to commemorate their remembrance; whilst many Heroes, who died in defence of their country, were instantly forgot, and not a stone erected to tell where they lay.

In fine, the laws and institutions, in authorising female solitude, stamped marriage with the idea of an inestimable treasure. But in Athens—fancy, a taste for the Fine Arts, an insatiable thirst for pleasure of every kind, seemed to revolt against the laws themselves; and Courtezans were called in as it were as auxiliaries to the manners and dispositions of the times. Vice, banished from domestic life, affected not the happiness of families, but Vice under a parental roof was ever pronounced criminal. By a strange and unaccountable whimsicalness, the male sex stood con-

fessedly

feffedly corrupted, whilft domeftic manners were exemplarily rigid. Courtezans were eftimated according to their
attractions, and what the French have
happily ftiled *agrémens*; whilft other
women laid no other claim to merit, than
what they were entitled to by their virtue.   From thefe various circumftances,
we may account for the honours which
Courtezans fo frequently received in
Greece, otherwife it would have been
difficult to conceive how fix or feven
Authors would have confecrated their
pens to celebrate them, how three of
the moft celebrated Painters had devoted
their pencils folely to pourtray them;
how feveral Grecian Poets had invoked
their Mufes to honour them: in a
word, it would be very difficult, otherwife, to affign a caufe, why the greateft
men fhould, with the keeneft avidity,
aim at being introduced into their company,

pany; that ASPASIA should be the sole Herald of Peace or War; or that PHRYNIA should have a statue of gold erected to her memory. The uninformed traveller approaching the Walls of *Athens*, observing at a distance this monument, fancies it is the tomb of MILTIADES or of PERICLES, or some Hero equally renowned; but upon his nearer approach, he is informed it is the Mausoleum of an Athenian Courtezan, whose memory is thus pompously blazoned. Of all the renowned Warriors that fought for their country in *Asia*, there is not one whose glorious deeds are commemorated with a monument, or whose ashes have ever been thought worthy of future panegyric. Such, however, were the honours and homage paid by that enthusiastic, voluptuous, and sensual people to the shrine of Beauty!

THIS

THIS sketch of the veneration in which Courtezans have been held by a nation esteemed the wisest and most learned of Antiquity, will, we hope, afford a sufficient apology for our having taken up the pen as Biographers of the present race of THAIS's, whose pictures, however, we shall endeavour to delineate with the crayons of Truth; and whilst we allow them every possible merit they can justly claim, we shall not hide their faults, their blemishes, their vices, or their crimes. In the preceding Volume we have displayed them all; in this we shall be equally impartial: then let the rigid Cynic, or the still more rigid Puritan, determine, whether this production may not be of more service than detriment to the rising generation; and whether the scenes we have here exhibited are not, upon the whole, greater incentives to Virtue than to Vice.

CHAP.

C H A P. XXIV.

CHARLOTTE's *fruitful Projects for rai-
sing fresh Female Recruits for her Nunnery. Her Success. Her Invitation to
a high luscious Banquet, in which she
personates Queen* OBEREA. *Her Improvement upon the Rites of* VENUS, *as
performed at* Otaheite. *A very descriptive and salacious Scene, founded on the
most orthodox Philosophy.*

WE are going to pay a final visit
to CHARLOTTE HAYES, before
she quits *King's-Place*; and as she was
resolved, ere she retired from business, to make some capital strokes, she
first began to recruit her Nunnery with
fresh Pieces, in two different ways. The
first was, by attending Register-Offices;
the

the second, by Advertisement. We shall give a specimen of both these operations.

CHARLOTTE dressed herself in a plain, simple manner, resembling the wife of a decent tradesman, and repaired to the different Register-Offices about town, inquiring for a young, healthful-looking woman, about twenty, whose chief employment was to attend upon a Lady who resided in her first floor. Sometimes she thought proper to make her lodger bed-ridden, at other times, a little out of her mind, however, the wages were very handsome, and above the common rate. By these means she would have frequently a score in a day call upon her. In order to carry this scheme into execution, she took a variety of lodgings in different parts of the town, and sometimes small houses ready

furnished;

furnished; as the character of her Nunnery in the neighbourhood, if enquired after, would have given the alarm, and prevented her accomplishing the design. When any decent girl with a good face applied, she always hired her for the Lady in the first floor, who was very ill, and could not see her. It was requisite that the servant should lie by her, as her infirmities were so great, that it was necessary to have an attendant near her all night.

THESE preliminaries being settled, as the maid-servants generally go to their places in the evening, the unsuspicious girl was shewn into a dark room, the Lady's eyes being so bad that she could not bear a light. At ten o'clock the house all retired to rest; but it was expedient, previous to this step, to have

some

some supper. The girl with, perhaps, a very keen appetite, was allowed to sup with the Landlady (CHARLOTTE), when a good substantial dish was brought forth, good strong ale, and, as it was the first night, and to shew her hospitality, would indulge her with a glass of wine. NANCY's spirits being thus elevated, she retires to bed to her supposed superannuated mistress—when, lo! the poor innocent girl finds herself, in her first sleep, in the arms of Lord C--N, Lord B----KE, or Colonel L----E. In vain she laments the fraud that has been played upon her; her outcries bring no one to her relief, and probably she yields to her fate, finding it inevitable, and solaces herself in the morning with a few guineas, and the perspective view of having a new gown, a pair of silver buckles, and a black silk cloak Being once broke in, there is no great difficulty in perfuading her to remove her quarters, and repair to the Nunnery in *King's-Place*, in order to make room for another victim, who is to be facrificed in the like manner.

WHEN a fufficient fupply from thefe refources was not produced, Advertifements in the Daily Papers often had the defired effect, and brought in numbers of pretty candidates (though unknowingly) for proftitution. Moft of thefe advertifements were of a ferious nature, and carried with them all the appearance of truth, fincerity, and a good place, for any young woman inclined to go to fervice. But fometimes CHARLOTTE would flourifh in the jocular ftile, at leaft fome of her friends for her; and even thefe ludicrous publications have inveigled the innocent and unguarded. One in particular appeared fome time ago,

ago, which was very laughable, and was aſcribed to GEORGE S———N.

"WANTED,

"A young Woman, under twenty, "who has had the ſmall-pox, and has "not been long in town, as a Maid- "Servant of all work, in a genteel fa- "mily. She muſt turn her hand to "every thing, as it is propoſed putting "her under a Man-Cook of ſkill and "eminence. She muſt get up in all "things, and even large ones occa- "ſionally, underſtand clear-ſtarching "without clapping, and know ſome- "thing of paſtry, at leaſt to make ſtand- "ing cruſt, and alſo preſerving fruit. "Good wages and proper encourage- "ment will be given, if ſhe proves "handy, and can eaſily conceive, ac- "cording to the inſtructions given her."

LUDICROUS.

LUDICROUS as this advertisement may appear, it had so much effect, as to produce at least half-a-dozen young women, who came in consequence to be hired, and soon were made to turn their hands to every thing.

By these schemes CHARLOTTE had new initiated a dozen fine wenches, all wholesome and blooming, into the Arcanum of the Nunnery; and she had now begun to train them for a new species of amusement for her noble and honourable guests. They had already gone through their exercises for near a fortnight, twice every day, when she dispatched a circular Card to all her best customers.

" MRS. HAYES presents her most
" respectful compliments to Lord ——,
" and takes the liberty to acquaint him,
" that to-morrow evening, precisely at
" seven,

" seven, a dozen beautiful Nymphs,
" unfullied and untainted, and who
" breathe health and nature, will per-
" form the celebrated rites of VENUS,
" as practiſed at *Otaheite*, under the
" inſtruction and tuition of Queen
" OBEREA; in which character Mrs.
" HAYES will appear upon this oc-
" caſion."

THAT the Reader may form a com-
petent idea of their exerciſes, we ſhall
give the following quotation from
Cook's Voyage, written by the celebrated Doctor Hawkeſworth.

" SUCH were our Matins," ſpeaking of
ſome religious Ceremonies performed by
the Indians in the morning. "Our Indians
" thought fit to perform Veſpers of a
" very different kind. A young man,
" ſix feet high, performed the Rites of
" VENUS

" VENUS with a little girl about eleven
" or twelve years of age, before several
" of our people, and a great number of
" the natives, without the least sense of
" its being indecent or improper, but,
" as appeared, in perfect conformity to
" the custom of the place. Among the
" spectators were several women of supe-
" rior rank, particularly Oberea, who
" may properly be said to have assisted
" at the ceremony; for they gave in-
" structions to the girl how to perform
" her part, which, young as she was,
" she did not seem much to stand in
" need of."

THE Reader will certainly not be dif-
pleased with Dr. Hawkesworth's comment upon the performance of these
Rites, as they are more than curious,
truly philosophical. He says,

" THIS

" THIS incident is not mentioned as
" an object of idle curiosity, but as it
" deserves consideration in determining,
" which has long been debated in philo-
" sophy, Whether the shame attending
" certain actions, which are allowed on
" all sides to be in themselves innocent,
" is implanted in nature, or superin-
" duced by custom? If it has its origin
" in custom, it will, perhaps, be found
" difficult to trace that custom, how-
" ever general, to its source: if in instinct,
" it will be equally difficult to discover
" for what cause it is subdued, or over-
" ruled among these people, in whose
" manners the least trace is to be found."
Hawkesworth's Voyages, Vol. II. p. 128.

MRS HAYES had certainly consulted
these pages with uncommon attention,
and she concluded, that shame upon similar occasions " was only superinduced
" by

" by cuftom ," and being fo much of a Natural Philofopher as to have fur- mounted all prejudices, fhe refolved not only to teach her Nuns all the Rites of VENUS as practifed at *Otaheite*, but to improve upon them, with the invention, fancy, and caprice of ARETIN , having taught them every one of his Poftures, in their former rehearfals, and in which they were already pretty expert.

UPON this *falacious Olympic*, fhe had no lefs than three-and-twenty Vifitors, confifting chiefly of the firft Nobility, fome Baronets, and but five Commoners.

No fooner had the clock ftruck feven, than the *Feftino* began. She had engaged a dozen of the moft athletic, and beft proportioned young men that could be procured ; fome of them Royal Aca- demic figures, and the reft well qualified for the fport. A large carpet being laid, and all the apparatus for the various attitudes into which the Votaries of VE-NUS were to appear, according to the ARETIN fyftem, being prepared—after the males had prefented each of their miftreffes with a Nail of at leaft twelve inches in length, in imitation of the prefents received by the Ladies of *Ota-heite* upon thefe occafions, giving the preference to a long Nail before any other compliment,—they entered upon their devotions, and went through all the various evolutions, according to the word of command of SANTA-CHARLOT-TA, with the gieateft dexterity, keeping the moft regular time, to the no fmall gratification of the lafcivious fpectators, fome of whom could fcarce refrain till the end of the *fpectacle*, before they were impetuous to perform a part in this Cy-prian game, which lafted near two hours,

I

and

and met with the higheſt applauſe from all preſent; Mrs. HAYES's directions being ſo judicious, that ſcarce a *manœuvre* was performed but with the greateſt exactitude and addreſs.

THE Rites being finiſhed, a collection was made for the Votaries of VENUS, and a handſome purſe ſubſcribed upon the occaſion. The male devotees being now diſmiſſed, the females remained, and moſt of them repeated the part they had ſo ſkilfully performed, with ſeveral of the ſpectators. Before they retired to reſt, the Champaign briſkly circulated, and Catches and Glees added to the merriment of the evening.

ABOUT four in the morning every Thais had been ſelected, and was retired to reſt; and ſoon after CHARLOTTE threw herſelf into the arms of the

Count,

Count, to practife, in part at leaft, what fhe was fo great a miftrefs of in theory.

Here we fhall drop the feftoon curtains for the prefent, and leave them all till about twelve at noon, to meet and breakfaft; as the fatigues of the evening muft have impofed the neceffary tax of fleep till at leaft that time.

CHAP.

CHAP. XXV.

Our last Audience and Farewell with CHAR-
LOTTE HAYES. *History of a certain
celebrated* Thais. *Outline of the History of the Three Sisters (not the* Parcæ).
Amours of NELLY ELLIOT. *Her Acquaintance with M. D——N. Forms
an Acquaintance with a Gamester upon
the Ton. The Vicissitudes of his Fortune,
and the melancholy Catastrophe of this
Historiette.*

WE left SANTA CHARLOTTA in the
arms of the Count, after her
uncommon carousal, in which the Rites
of VENUS were so peculiarly celebrated.
As we did not chuse to interrupt her that
night during her repose, we deferred
till this moment taking a final leave of
her, which we are compelled to do, as

C 3   she

she at this period took a final leave of the World, in her public capacity of Lady Abbess, Duenna, Procuress, and even SANTA CHARLOTTA. She had, by the stratagems we have pointed out for inveigling innocent girls, her fertile imagination of hiring them to the best advantage, and her eccentric genius of exhibiting uncommon feats of love, by this time realized at least twenty thousand pounds: she therefore resolved no longer to disturb herself with the toils of business, or the bustle of Nocturnal Revels.

HAVING thus dispatched CHARLOTTE HAYES, we shall now pay a visit to a Lady in *Newman-Street*, not far from the *Middlesex-Hospital*, and as we are sure of meeting with a genteel and polite reception, the Reader, let him be of what

rank

rank or dignity he may, need not be afhamed of accompanying us.

THE Lady in queftion is Mifs NELLY ELLIOT, otherwife Mrs HAMILTON (an adopted name, for reafons we fhall hereafter affign). Mifs NELLY is the daughter of an Officer of rank in the Army. She, with two other elder fifters, were brought up in a very genteel manner, and received an education fuitable to their rank. In their juvenile days their refidence was at *Chelfea*; and her two Sifters fhone at the Affembly there as capital toafts. They were fine fhewy girls, tall and graceful; and as they dreffed to the height of the fafhion, they had many danglers and admirers, but when the grand queftion came to be agitated about fortune, there was a conftant demur.—" The ELLIOTS are " clever wenches—but there is no mo-

C 4 " ney,"

·" ney," fays one.—" The Devil-they
" have not!" obferves another; " then
" what pretenfions have they to huf-
" bands?—They muft veer about, and
" look out for a fettlement: men
" are not to be caught now-a-days with
" painting bubbles, and a gauze-hand-
" kerchief half fpread over them You
" know, JACK, we can have as fine a
" Piece as any upon the Town for a
" guinea, and *Variety* is my motto."—
" Faith, you are right, WILL, the EL-
" LIOTS muft knock under, as there are
" no fpankers in the cafe —I think I'll
" propofe taking one of them into keep-
" ing."—" And egad, JACK, I'll try the
" other." Thus was the deftiny of the
handfome Sifters fettled and deter-
mined.

NELLY, the Heroine of this ftory,
was all the while out of the mefs;—fhe
had

had never yet fhewn her face at the Affembly, or fcarcely at Church. The
reafon was neither more nor lefs than
this ·—The eldeft fifter being purfe-
bearer, in the abfence of her father,
who was abroad, applied all the money
fhe poffibly could to the decorating of her
own dear perfon, but as it was neceffary
to have a companion, her next fifter was
permitted to accompany her in public,
but in a drefs far inferior to her own—
wearing, for the greater part, little more
than her caft-off clothes. What then
was to become of poor NELLY? Her
wardrobe muft be none of the choiceft,
as it confifted of the third and laft edition of her eldeft fifter's caft-off apparel.
Thus mortified and defpifed, fhe had
been for fome time meditating an elopement, and only waited for a favourable
opportunity to decamp in a decent man-

ner,

ner; but her fifters became now fo extremely peevifh and intolerably tyrannical
towards her, occafioned partly by their
natural ill-temper, and partly fiom the
ill fuccefs of the artillery of their charms,
which they had now played off in public
for near two years without producing
any other effect than an offer of being
taken into keeping, that fhe refolved to
defer no longer making her efcape. Accordingly, one evening, when her fifters
were gone to *Ranelagh*, fhe dreffed herfelf in one of her eldeft fifter's beft
facques and petticoats, and, in fhort,
equipped herfelf from top to toe in her
apparel, and fet off *à la fourdine*. She
repaired to the houfe of a maid-fervant
who had formerly lived with them, and
was now married to a reputable tradefman. This perfon had often commife-
rated NELLY's pitiable fituation, and
wifhed

wished it was in her power to afford her relief She accordingly presented NELLY a welcome asylum, who remained with her some weeks There was another lodger in the house, who passed for a modest woman, but there was reason to suspect that she was supported by a gentleman who often visited her, and passed for a relation.

WITH this Lady NELLY went one evening to *Marybone Gardens*, where they were presently joined by her nominal relation and another Gentleman. The latter paid great regard to NELLY; said many civil things, and made some indirect overtures of an amorous kind. NELLY was not in the least displeased with these compliments, and upon her return home, was very inquisitive to know who this gentleman was; when

she

fhe learnt that he was a man of fortune,
and reckoned very generous to the Ladies. The information greatly pleafed
her, and difperfed a melancholy that had
for fome days preyed upon her, occafioned by the difagreeable profpect before
her, and fome hints thrown out by her
hoftefs, that it was time to think of looking out for another lodging.

THE very next day both Gentlemen
paid her acquaintance a vifit, and NEL-
LY was requefted to be of the party.
Nothing could have given her more
pleafure, efpecially as it was propofed
to make a trip that evening, which
was remarkably fine, to *Vauxhall.* In
the ccurfe of a *tête à-tête* which NELLY's
admirer had with her in one of the foli-
tary walks, he told her, " He flattered
" himfelf he had not been guilty of
" any

" any impertinence, in taking a lodging
" for her that very day in an airy part
" of the town; and begged she would
" repair thither the next day and take
" poffeffion." By this unexpected ftroke
NELLY was taken by furprize, and
without hefitation gave her affent to his
requeft. This once done, fhe had, as it
were, ratified all the preliminaries of his
moft fanguine wifhes.

THE night paffed with great merriment and hilarity; the Champaign circulated, and NELLY's fpirits were fo
elevated, as to be ripe for any frolic
whatever. This pleafant fcene continued
till paft three in the morning, when, as it
was agreed on all hands that the Ladies
could gain no admiffion at their lodgings,
and it being a moft delightful morning, it
was pronounced a fin to fleep. A trip to
Windfor

Windsor was refolved upon, and by day-break they were difpofed of in two poft-chaifes. NELLY neceffarily fell to Mr. D——N's lot, as his partner; and he failed not to improve the opportunity of cultivating as intimate an acquaintance with her as poffible. In a word, every thing had taken place but confummation; and a convenient retreat feemed all that was wanting for the completion of Mr. D——N's happinefs. Judge Reader, if it was long before this was obtained.

THEY had no fooner alighted at *Windfor*, and ordered breakfaft, than Mr. D——N, who was well acquainted with the houfe, conducted his Enamorata to a pleafant fummer-houfe at the end of the garden, that appeared confecrated to love and blifs.

HERE

HERE we fhall leave them for fome time, to pay their devotions (which were very fervent on both fides) to the Cyprian Goddefs. Breakfaft being announced, they returned; when NELLY's blufhes too plainly indicated the flurry of her fpirits, the agitation of her heart, and the influence of modefty. However, as no fuggeftions were thrown out to difconcert her, the breakfaft paffed over, with little other converfation than trite obfervations on the finenefs of the weather, and their future deftination for dinner.

UPON their return to town, Mr. D———N conducted NELLY to her new apartments; made her a handfome prefent to purchafe what fhe had occafion for; and fettled an allowance of five guineas a week for her maintenance.

In

In this fituation NELLY remained for near three months, during which time fhe not only was equipt with a good ftock of genteel clothes, but fome jewels and trinkets, and was fo good an œconomift as to fave near fifty guineas. Notwith-ftanding the cruel treatment fhe had received at the hands of her eldeft fifter, fhe thought it but juft to make her fome return for the facque and other things fhe had purloined from her, and accordingly fent her a fine piece of filk, fome lace, and other valuable things, to fupply her lofs.

CLOYED with repeated gratifications, Mr. D——n, at the end of this period, took a French leave of her, after giving her a Bank-note, not knowing fhe had made any provifion for herfelf out of her weekly allowance. Mortified to the ut-moft degree at this defertion, fhe foon

found

found fome confolation in thinking fhe was placed above want, that fhe was not pregnant, and her flattering glafs told her, there were plenty of conquefts in ftore for her.

In this opinion fhe reforted to all public places, and endeavoured to fecure another Paramour, who would fupport her as elegantly, at leaft, as Mr. D——N had done. In the courfe of this purfuit fhé met with a Mr. S——N, who paffed for a man of fortune; and fo he certainly was, in one fenfe of the word, for he relied entirely on the Blind Goddefs for his fupport. He figured away at the rate of more than a thoufand a-year; but this was to be extracted from two cubical bones, vulgarly called Dice. Thefe bones were fometimes fo very obdurate, as to turn a deaf ear to all his intreaties, his vows, his oaths;

and

and that critical expreſſion, " Seven is,
" the main," has often ſent him home
pennyleſs. However, when he had a
favourable run of luck, no man was
more generous, and NELLY found herſelf at one time in poſſeſſion of ſeven
hundred pounds, a valuable ſide-board
of plate, and ſome jewels of conſiderable value. But alas! this Elyſium was
ſoon changed—the ſcene ſhifted—a dark
and dreary view preſented itſelf—rocks
and inacceſſible mountains formed the
depicted road for NELLY now to travel. Without a metaphor——in one
week all the caſh, all the jewels, all the
plate, were transferred at the hazard-
table, and S——N was not maſter of a
ſhilling. Poor NELLY's furniture ſoon
took the ſame route; her clothes followed, and to complete the cataſtrophe,
S——N was a ſhort time after in the
King's-Bench priſon at his taylor's ſuit.

NOT-

Notwithstanding S——n's misfortunes, Nelly had still a *penchant* for him—as he had many valuable qualities, and had he been of real fortune, he would probably have shone an ornament to Society She did not defert him in his diftrefs; and though fhe was under fuch pungent diftrefs, as to be compelled to go into company for her fupport, fhe fhared with him the fpoils of her charms, and maintained him, if not in a luxuriant, at leaft in a decent manner, for fome months, in the Bench. At length, alas! her variegated amours teftified a diforder, which had arrived at fuch a pitch of virulence as to compel her to have recourfe to the *hauts remedes.*

CHAP.

C H A P. XXVI.

NELLY ELLIOT's *most melancholy Situa-*
tion. Writes to her Sister for Relief—
That Lady's Answer being the most
extraordinary Epistle of the kind, per-
haps, ever penned. Is relieved by an
old Acquaintance. Renews her brilliant
Appearance in the Gay World Makes
Acquaintance with a very worthy Gen-
tleman, who pays her due Respect. His
Misfortunes involve her into Difficulties
Her future Career, and present Plan.

WE left poor NELLY ELLIOT, in
our last Chapter, in a most de-
plorable condition —- without friends,
without money, without health, destitute of all the comfort, all the solace
of life; and the only man she esteemed,
immured in durance vile. What a
complicated

complicated picture of calamity! And
yet NELLY was a profeffed Woman of
Pleafure,—but it is not extraordinary,
as this is the lot of nine-tenths of the
Women of Pleafure all over Europe.

LET us, however, pay her a friendly
vifit, for the fake of old acquaintance.
NELLY had, in this lamentable flate,
written a very moving letter to Mr.
D——N, depicting her moft melancholy
cafe, and probably, if he had been in
town, he might have afforded her fome
temporary relief, but he was at his
feat in *Derbyfhire*, at a great diftance
from the capital. Her wants and diftrefs were now fo alarming, that the
nurfe who attended her through mere
charity, and who had pledged every
thing fhe had been poffeffed of, except
the clothes upon her back, to relieve our
unfortunate Heroine, was under the
moft

most violent apprehensions that she
would fall a sacrifice to the want of mere
necessaries.—In this cruel dilemma, the
good old Samaritan persuaded her to
write to her sister for some assistance.
She accordingly did, as well as she was
able, in her present emaciated state.
This letter produced nothing but the
following curious answer.

" ASTONISHED as I am at your
" insolence, to address me in a letter, in
" your present infamous situation, with
" all the just calamities of Heaven,
" which you yourself have brought
" upon your head—I nevertheless think
" it my duty, as once your sister—mor-
" tifying reflection !—to give you some
" advice that may save your soul, by
" repentance, from everlasting destruc-
" tion. As to your mortal part, the
" sooner it pays the inevitable debt
" of

" of Nature, the better for yourfelf—
" the better for the world. Such exe-
" crable beings crawling upon the face
" of the earth, are noxious to the fight,
" are obnoxious to Society, and bane-
" ful to mankind. You have now ftill
" leifure to reflect on your unhappy ftate
" —and confider yourfelf as the fole ar-
" chitect of your mifery. What could
" induce you to follow fuch a courfe of
" life? Had you the example of any
" of your relations for fuch a conduct?
" No—thank Heaven! we are all vir-
" tuous and immaculate. You alone
" have tarnifhed the chaftity of our fa-
" mily reputation. In you the crime,
" the vicious crime, is lefs excufeable,
" than in many unfortunate females who
· have been blinded by love, and fe-
" duced by artful men: but you have
" no fuch apology in your favour.
" Without any particular object to
" tempt

" tempt or allure you—without either
" the plea of the tender paffion, or fe-
" duction, you wantonly—moft wan-
" tonly facrificed your virgin purity to
" luft—abominable luft. By fuch a pro-
" cedure, you have placed yourfelf be-
" neath the brute creation.—They have
" not reafon for their guide. inftinct
" alone directs them. Think then,
" wretch, how thou art fallen! You
" have deftroyed all ties of kindred,
" and broken down every fence of
" friendfhip. To your own pungent
" feelings, if you are not loft to every
" fenfe of fhame, I now confign you,
" or elfe I fhall rave my rage is kindled,
" therefore trouble me no more with
" your naufeous, fulfome—I had almoft
" faid, contaminating epiftles; for you
" will never hear more from her who
" was once your Sifter."

Ir

IF this letter required any comment, the additional diftrefs it threw poor NELLY into, could alone depict it; but it would be a tafk far above the powers of the pen of the Writer of this Chapter, who was an eye-witnefs of the violent emotions of her mind upon this occafion, to attempt delineating it.

AFTER having betrayed myfelf into this acknowledgment, I muft for the prefent fpeak in the fingular number. I immediately relieved her moft alarming neceffities, and procured her fuch future affiftance, as not only removed every apprehenfion of her falling a facrifice to want, or being debarred from fuch medicinal advice as her cafe required.

To avoid eulogium, *we* fhall now refume our wonted *plurality*.

No sooner had NELLY recovered her health, than she re-appeared in the Gay World with her usual elegance and vivacity, and she soon after formed an alliance with a gentleman then well known in polite life, and remarkable for the darkness of his complexion But let it not be suggested that he was a SOUBISE: No—he was a Creole, with very regular features, his person remarkably well proportioned, tall and athletic This was the Mr. H——N whose name she has ever since adopted. No sooner had this connexion taken place, than she was invited home to his house in *Salisbury-Street,* in the *Strand,* where she presided, and did the honours of the table in so polite a manner, as to distinguish the gentlewoman.

THUS provided for in an elegant line of life, NELLY evinced that no woman

deserved

deferved more the attention and affidui-
ties of a man of tafte and refinement
(which certainly Mr H——n was) than
herfelf. He had a very handfome fortune, and lived up to it, after having
made NELLY a fettlement of fifty pounds
a year He was guilty of no extravagance that would have affected his eftate,
nor was fhe guilty of any unneceffary
expence beyond the rules of prudence,
but unfortunately he was addicted to
play, and he fell into the hands of a fett
of fharpers, who ftile themfelves Gentlemen, but who, in fact, are far greater
er pick-pockets than the unhappy con-
victs who are fentenced to ballaft-heav
ing for taking unlawfully a handkerchief, or even a watch. Thefe nefarious villains, under the mafk of friendfhip, and the affumed title of men of
rank and fortune, decoy the unwary into their wiles, and by a variety of ftra-

tagems.

tagems, and deep-laid artifices, plun-
der and ruin every one that falls into
their clutches. This was the fatal situation of Mr. H——N, who in the course
of a few months was compelled to
mortgage his estate, discontinue house-
keeping, and go abroad to live a retired
and recluse life, whilst his fortune was
at nurse. In consequence of this disaster,
poor NELLY was once more thrown upon the wide world, and compelled to
begin her game over again, when she
thought, according to her own manner
of expressing it, " she was home to a
" hole."

FOR some time NELLY still retained
her importance; and she was unwilling
to submit to return, what is called, " in-
" to company." But that all-powerful
word *Necessity* soon compelled her,

and

and we find her upon *Harrison's* * real Lift, a fhort time after, in *Rathbone-Place*.

NELLY was not, however, in this degraded ftation for any length of time. She found friends to affift her, particularly a very worthy young gentleman in the upholftery branch, who furnifhed, in a very genteel manner, the houfe fhe now lives in.

HAVING conducted her to the prefent agreeable fituation fhe refides in, the Reader will expect that fome account fhould be given of the manner in which

---

* An annual impofition is yearly obtruded upon the Public, as *Harris's* Lift of Grizettes, but it is conftantly more erroneous in the Contents than the Title-page, for no fuch man as *Harris* (as he is called) a Pimp, now, or probably ever did exift.

fhe

she supports herself.——Mrs. HAMIL-
TON's house may properly be stiled a
House of Intrigue, rather than a Nunnery Some of the finest come-at able women in the purlieus of this metropolis,
occasionally frequent it. She is far from
being of a mercenary disposition, like
the other Lady Abbesses: she would rather give a genteel treat to a joyous, con-
vivial party, than receive one from a
dull, phlegmatic sett, who promote
spleen, in proportion as they expend
their money   Hence it is, that some of
the most Choice Spirits, and men of
learning, wit, and humour, frequent
her house; not so much for the sake of
gratifying any lascivious passion, as for
the pleasure of good company, and passing
a few hours in agreeable society.   Here
it was that Mrs MITCHELL's ridiculous
Motto was first criticised.—A certain
gentleman of NELLY's particular acquaintance

quaintance being afked his opinion of
the infcription, faid, it was truly worthy
of an Old Bawd, who had been impofed
upon by fome male pandar, defirous o.
paffing for a fcholar, and had approved
himfelf a mere pimp in learning, and
only qualified to proftitute Horace, as
he did the nominal Veftals of her Seminary. My ever revered Bard would
have been fhocked to have feen

IN MEDIO TUTISSIMUS,

without IBIS being fubjoined.

FROM this fpecimen of Mrs. HAMIL-
TON's friends, acquaintance, and vifitors,
the Reader will be enabled to form fome
idea of the complexion of the frequenters
of her houfe in general. But in faying
this, we do not pretend to affert, that
this is the region of Platonic Love: no
woman is a greater fenfualift in the amorous

passion

paffion than NELLY herfelf. It is true, that fhe has a favourite *man*, or rather fhe is the favourite of a very *good-natured man*, who has fome connection with the Theatres; but we will not pretend to fay fhe is as chafte as *Penelope*, and unravels in the night the work of the day, in his abfence. No, NELLY is too fincere to lay claim to any kindred with Diana; all fhe aims at is to keep up appearances, and fupport the dignity of the gentle-woman.

In our next Chapter, our Readers will be introduced to fome of her female vifitors, and thereby be enabled to form a judgment of the entire plan of her houfe, which, of the kind, may be pro-nounced one of the moft eligible in that quarter of the Town.

CHAP.

CHAP XXVII.

History of Mrs. BR——DL——Y.
*Her Marriage Her coming upon the
Stage. Her Connexions with Lords*
M—H *and* B—E. *Makes an Alliance
with the Duke of* D——T : *The Reason
of its not being permanent. Frames an
Acquaintance with the Macaroni Bricklayer. History of the Lovely* CHAR-
LOTTE S—RS. *Treachery of her Guar-
dians, and the Effects of her Condescen-
sion.*

THE first upon NELLY's list of
femmes moitié entretenues, who
frequented her sprightly rendezvous,
was Mrs. BR—DL—Y. This Lady is
tall and genteel, remarkably fair, with
fine

fine blue eyes and flaxen locks. Before her late fit of illnefs, fhe was pronoun-ced uncommonly handfome, and in pro-portion as fhe recovers her health, fhe renovates her charms. In her youth fhe made a foolifh match, without confult-ing her heart or her judgment: Ma-trimony had fo many charms in her eyes, that fhe forgot to make a felection in the choice of a hufband; and Mr. TWEEDLEDUM and TWEEDLEDEE TWEEDLEDEED her into the connubial knot But though mufic has charms to foothe the favage breaft, it had not powers fufficient to enrapture a female, almoft angelic. He *hum-ftrummed* to no fort of purpofe, and fhe thought his notes were jarring and out of tune: he had not, with the Poet, found out

———— The key which paffions move
To ravifh'd fenfe, and play a world in love.

This

This idle, girlifh match Mrs. B—y foon
difcovered, was no way confonant to her
mode of thinking, her ideas were refined, her notions elegant, and her difpofition directly oppofite to vulgarifm. On
the contrary, Mr. TWEEDLEDUM was
never happy but in a pot-houfe, affociating with low Actors, and ftill lower
Mechanics. How then could it be expected, that they fhould live long together upon an, amicable footing ? The
truth is, fhe had taken fo complete a
difguft to her *caro fpofo*, that fhe only
waited for a favourable opportunity to
throw off the trammels of wedlock. It
was prudent, however, previous to fuch
a ftep, to lay fome plan for her future
fupport. She had a tafte for acting,
and fung very prettily ; thefe fhe imagined would be recommendations
for her, to obtain a falary at leaft
fufficient for her maintenance She ac-

cordingly

cordingly applied to the late Mr. FOOTE; who, whether he was prejudiced in her favour, from the agreeableness of her perfon, or her theatrical abilities,— this much is certain, that he engaged her at a decent falary, and fhe made her firft appearance in the character of Lucy in the Beggar's Opera. Whether intimidated at facing, for the firft time, a brilliant and numerous audience, or dreading the cenfure of profeffed critics, fhe did not acquit herfelf fo well as might have been wifhed: She, neverthelefs, fung the airs with tafte, and met with confiderable applaufe. If this exhibition did not eftablifh her character as a firft rate Dramatic Performer, it excited the attention of every male beholder, to know who fhe was; and in a few days fhe had many propofals made her of an amorous kind. Lords M—H

and

and B—K℮ were rivals upon this occafion; and if the voice of Fame may be
credited, fhe was not unkind to either of
them. Be this as it may, thefe amours
weie but of a tranfient date. She foon
fucceeded NANCY PAR—ONS, in the
arms of the Duke of D———T; and
could fhe have bowled his Grace out at
cricket, as eafily as fhe had done NAN-
CY out of the *ruelle*, fhe probably might
have kept in ftill, and attained the laft
notch of hei ámbition: But it was her
misfortune never to have wielded a
batt, and his Grace thought it a difgrace to have any connexion, male or
female, with any one that was not a profeffed cricketer. This, in fome meafure, accounts for his late intrigue with
Lady D——Y, who, it feems, can handle
a batt, and knock the balls about, with
almoft any Peer in England.

FOOTE,

FOOTE, towards the clofe of the feafon, made love to her himfelf; but fearful that fhe fhould bring forth a boy
with a wooden leg, fhe declined his addreffes: The confequence was, being
ftruck off the lift of his performers, and
fhe never after appeared upon the ftage.

A VARIETY of lovers now prefented
themfelves, and in the courfe of thefe
purfuits fhe made acquaintance with
Mrs HAMILTON Here it was fhe firft
faw the Macaroni Bricklayer, as he is
ftiled in the print-fhops. The franknefs
of his behaviour, added to the opennefs
of his countenance, his athletic and
manly form, and his generofity, all united to prejudice her ftrongly in his favour,
and fhe readily liftened to the propofals
of a man, for whom fhe entertained fo
great a partiality. In a word, a few
days only elapfed before fhe confented

to

to live with him, and promised never to admit the addresses of any other, as long as he behaved to her in the manner she had the greatest reason to expect. Since that period this connexion has subsisted, and there are grounds to believe, that her fidelity is equal to his affection for her.

WE shall for the present leave the Macaroni Bricklayer and Mrs. BR—D—Y to enjoy themselves without interruption in each other's arms, as we think them as eligible a *tête-à-tête* as any within the bills of mortality, for though he may mount the ladder in the morning to inspect the covering of the Attic story, he never yet interrupted a poet in the midst of flogging Pegasus for a happy thought and a dinner, nor did he ever give orders for the untiling the roof of a protection-vender in the diplomatic

matic line, becaufe he was feven years in arrears with his landlord, and could not be ejected from the premifes : No, fuch deeds are left for other bricklayers than our friend and favourite the *Macaroni Trowellift*, though *Darly* has endeavoured to make him ridiculous in every print-fhop window, as well as in his own, in this Metropolis. No—his generous mind *foars* above fuch mean attempts, and he would rather cure a fmoaky chimney, two cubits about the roof, than interrupt *genius*, or diftrefs *embaffy*.

THE lovely CHARLOTTE S——RS may next be introduced with propriety, at NELLY's. If her good fenfe kept pace with her beauty, fhe would be a paragon of excellence ; but Nature feems to beftow her gifts in fome degree, to bring all mankind upon a par. In our

fex,

fex, generally fpeaking, Herculean vigour is feldom accompanied with the
wifdom of a Solomon, or the philofophy
of a Socrates. Xantippe certainly had
fome latent charms, or elfe Providence,
was d——n'd cruel to her, to form her
fuch a fcold, and not in fome degree
counterbalance this almoft intolerable
defect. Perhaps Socrates neglected family duty.—He certainly vifited the moft
celebrated Thais's of Athens, and it is
enough to make any woman fcold, to
fee a hufband go aftray, and neglect her
charms, real or imaginary. But why
this digreffion? I have not read *Triftram
Shandy* for thefe feven years and more;
he was once the moft fafhionable author
that ever wrote; but, like moft other
fafhions, the reading of Shandy is as
much obfolete, as reading the Bible by
the Coterie, or any of the Nunneries
within

within the purlieus of St James's, Marybone, or Piccadilly.—I therefore cannot possibly have caught (lately, at least, and the cure must have been eradicated ere now) the episodic contagion : For which reason I again embrace the lovely CHARLOTTE S——RS, and shall now stick to her, till I, and perhaps the Reader, may be cloyed of her.

MISS CHARLOTTE S——RS was the daughter of a Country Gentleman, who died whilst she was still in her infancy. Her mother had paid that natural forfeit some years before. A guardian was appointed for her, who, under the disguise of religion, and a puritanic life, had so ingratiated himself with Mr. S—RS, that he thought RAWL—NS but a few removes from a Saint —and a young Saint was what he almost adored ; for R——NS, at this time, was but just

come

come of age. He had, notwithstanding, already fquandered away the greateft part of his fortune, which had been
very confiderable; but as thefe extrava-
gancies were committed in the capital,
and he had not mortgaged his eftate, tho'
he had borrowed, when a minor, confiderable fums upon the moft ufurious
terms, in granting annuities, his diftreffes were unknown in Mr. S——————RS's
neighbourhood. But no fooner had he
become the guardian of Mifs S————RS,
than he paid off thefe annuities with
her fortune; and by keeping her in a
conftant ftate of ignorance with regaid
to the precife ftate of her affairs, as fhe
advanced to maturity, he judged it expedient to play a double game. Mifs
S————RS having the moft implicit faith
in all that R————s faid, when he told
her, " it was now time to reveal to her
" the

" the dying words of Mr. S——rs; and
" that with his laft accents he energe-
" tically faid, Be not only a father, but a
" hufband to my daughter, for no man
" can deferve her fo well as yourfelf,"
fhe readily believed the affertion, and
having no predilection for any other
man, innocently, or rather foolifhly
confented to give him her hand. Having fo far gained his point in this nefarious bufinefs, he thought there would
be no difficulty in fpeedily accomplifh-
ing it. He accordingly took her in an
unguarded moment, and throwing himfelf at her feet, declared, " His paffion
" was fo great for her, that he could no
" longer live without her; that he
" would marry her that inftant.—But,
" my dear CHARLOTTE, what would
" the cenforious world fay? They would
" fay, that I had taken advantage of
" your

" your youth and inexperience, to make
" myfelf mafter of your beautiful per-
" fon and your fortune. Think what
" I feel in fuch a dilemma! Confider me,
" therefore, as your guardian, your fin-
" cere friend, and your moft loving
" hufband, for fuch I am, and then re-
" fufe me, if you can, the rights I de-
" mand." Saying this, he almoft de-
voured her with kiffes. Thus taken by
furprize, fhe had not the power to refift, and fhe yielded to his brutal luft,
without knowing that fhe was guilty of
any crime.

THEY lived together about two years
upon this clandeftine footing. At the
end of that period, he was carried off by
a putrid fever His brother ftept in,
he dying inteftate, and took poffeffion of
the fragments of R——NS's fortune; as

to her's, that had been appropriated long before.

Thus thrown upon the world friendless and pennyless, what road could an innocent, ignorant girl pursue? Beautiful and young, she soon fell a prey to Mrs. Pendergast, who made a considerable property of her, before she was taken into keeping by Lord C—sf—t. In this situation she now moved, when she paid her visits to Nelly Elliot.— But, notwithstanding this Lady is a very agreeable and entertaining companion, the Reader will probably think we have made our visit to her too long, we shall therefore here take our leave of her for the present.

CHAP.

CHAP. XXVIII.

Sketch of the juvenile Adventures of Mrs. N—n. Plans, in Conjunction with Mr. N——n, a Nunnery in Wardour-Street. Progress of her Undertaking. Various Efforts to improve her Plan. Schemes of Seduction. A Coup de Maitreffe in an original Line. Plans the Ruin of two beautiful young Ladies. A descriptive Scene, and the Event. Consequences of this Procedure.

THE Editor prefents his moft refpectful compliments to Mrs. N—n, and intreats her pardon for having neglected to take proper notice of her in the firft Edition he will, however, endeavour to make her fome

amends,

amends, by paying her due attention in this place.

MRS. NELSON is a Lady who in the early part of life was confidered as a Toaft of fome eminence, and at length yielded to the influence of her paffions in the arms of Captain W——N. He was for fome time conftant to her; but another charmer coming in his way, he deferted this Lady, and left her to roam at large. She foon became a come-at-able piece at HADDOCK's, and the reft of the Bagnios about the Garden. When fhe found hei chaims were upon the decline, and that her conftitution was fomewhat impaired by irregularities and too frequent vifits, fhe liftened to a Mr. N——N, who hinted to her, it would be prudent to ietire from public life, fell out of HARRISON's Lift, adopt his name, and comnence Lady Abbefs.

He

He added, he had fome credit with an Upholfterer; and from the knowledge and experience fhe had obtained in the *regular courfe of her profeffion*, united to his fkill and judgment, drawn from real life, and a variety of vocations he had purfued, he judged that the fcheme would not only be practicable, but prove very fuccefsful.

Mrs N—n admired his plan, and readily engaged in it: accordingly a genteel houfe was taken in *Wardour-Street, Soho,* the corner of *Holland-Street,* and in a fhort time fitted up and furnifhed in a very elegant manner. It was neceffary previoufly to lay in a ftock of Nuns, which were foon procured from various quarters; and we accordingly foon found NANCY BR—N, MARIA S—s, LUCY F—SHER, and CHARLOTTE M—RTIN, almoft inftantly

engaged.

engaged. Thefe were all very agreeable girls, though fome of them had been upon the town for a confiderable time, but it was expedient to be provided with *Recruits* for immediate ufe, as Mrs. NELSON propofed lying in wait for more delicate game, whenever opportunities occurred, refolving affiduoufly to feize every one that offered.

HER fecretary and nominal hufband was now employed to write circular letters to fuch noblemen and men of fortune as were known to frequent Mrs GOADBY's, &c. In a few days fhe had innumerable vifitors. Lord M—H, Lord D—NE, Lord B—KE, the Duke of D—T, Count H—G, Lord F—TH, Lord H—N, and an eftimable catalogue of rich Commoners, paid their compliments to her, but they generally complained that her goods were rather ftale, and

and she was frequently obliged to send out for other Ladies in order to please her customers · by this means her profits were diminished, and the credit and reputation of her house rather called into question. She accordingly exerted her genius, and it was pretty fertile in the arts of seduction, to obtain some *genuine vestals*, for whom she might demand her own price. Mrs. NELSON now became a constant visitor at the Register-Office and Statute-Hall, and attended the inns whenever the waggons and stage coaches were expected to arrive, where, by her artful insinuations, and pretences of getting the rustic wenches places and the like, she soon obtained as pretty an assortment of fresh goods as could be found in London.

MRS. NELSON's triumph now began over all her rivals, and Mrs. GOADBY, in particular, became very jealous of her, and in order to put her Nunnery upon a footing with Mrs. NELSON's, she made the tour of England one summer in the Stages, and was very successful in catering for her guests, upon the meeting of Parliament the ensuing winter.

THE intelligence Mrs N—— received upon this head, so far from making her despond, excited a stronger emulation in her to outvie Mrs. GOADBY She accordingly once more set her invention to work; and having a little smattering of French, and being a tolerable tambour and needle worker in her youth, upon seeing an advertisement for a Boarding-School Teacher, made application, and obtained the place. As it was not her design to remain here any time, she did not attempt conveying

4   much

much inftruction to the young Ladies with refpect to the improvement of theu morals, or their education; but, on the contrary, fhe endeavoured to vitiate their minds, by occafional hints of the blifsful enjoyments in the ca- reffes of a fine young fellow, and the folly and prejudice of thinking it any crime to give way to their fenfual paf- fions. To this end fhe put into their hands every book, that fhe judged would tend to awaken their lafcivious inclina- tons, and inftil the moft lafcivious ideas: *Memoirs of a Woman of Plea--* *fire, The Adventures of Mr. F——— in* *Petticoats,* and feveral other produc- tions of this kind were fecretly com- municated to them, and they read them with avidity. When fhe judged fhe had fufficiently wrought upon their paffions, and found the amorous flame to burn with anguifh and infuperable

E 3   desire;

desire, one day, under pretence of taking an ailing, she paid a visit with two
of the finest girls in the school, between
fixteen and seventeen, at her own house
in *Wardour Street* These young Ladies
names were Miss W——ms and Miss
J——nes, both of very good families.

Mrs. N—— had previously planted
Lord B—— and Mr. G——, to be ready
for receiving these amiable Visitors.
They no sooner alighted, than a cold
collation was prepared, with fruit and
sweetmeats in abundance. She informed the young Ladies that it was a Relation's house, where she could make
free, and intreated them to observe no
ceremony. The young Ladies accordingly enjoyed the repast with much
satisfaction, and were induced to drink
a glass or two of wine, which put them

in

in uncommon fpirits. Mrs. N——
now thought it was time to introduce
the Gentlemen; and though they were
already in the houfe, a rap at the door
announced their arrival. On entering
the room, they apologized for their in-
trufion, and the young Ladies were at
firft much alarmed, but the politenefs
of the Gentlemen foon furmounted
their alarms, and an agreeable converfation enfued upon a variety of topics.

It now began to grow late, and the
young Ladies became fomewhat uneafy
how they fhould get home, having to
go beyond *Kenfington*; but mufic was
immediately introduced, and a dance
propofed; which fo intoxicated the poor
girls, who were paffionately fond of dancing, that they now forgot all *time* but
the *time* they were to keep in a Cotillon.

In

In a word, they continued dancing till midnight, and the negus, which was remarkably strong, was very briskly circulated, under pretence of its being a warm night, of course it failed not to operate, together with the pastime, and the uncommon assiduity of their partners made them forget danger, and almost court destruction.

About two in the morning they retired to rest together, and whilst they were undressing, they could not help comparing notes concerning the elegance of the persons, and the gentility of the behaviour of their partners. Miss W—ms vowed she wished she had Lord B——— all night in her arms; and Miss J—ves declared she believed she should dissolve in bliss, if Mr. G—— were in bed with her. The lovers were in hearing.

hearing, and broke in upon them, saying, that it was impoffible to refufe fuch paffionate invitations, and that they muft be more than mortal if they could liften to fuch extatic declarations, and not offer their fervices.

THE young Ladies were now both upon the point of getting into bed, having nothing but their fhifts on; when Mr G—— feizing Mifs J—NES in his arms, carried her to a bed in an adjacent room, and left Lord B—— mafter of the field with Mifs W—MS. They had gone too far to recede, and their fate became now inevitable.

WE fhall for the prefent drop the curtain, and fuppofe the lovers and the beauteous nymphs as happy as their fituations

would

would permit; that unbounded bliss prevailed till morning——

" But then To-morrow!
" Aye, there's the Rub."

How to return to school—how to apologize for their abfence! Fain would they have prevailed with their Governefs to have re-conducted them to their Miftrefs, and framed fome plaufible apology for their playing the truant. With tears and intreaties they implored her arbitration; but Mrs. N—n's game was now up at K—n, fhe had the cards entirely in her own hand, and had already played a *fans prendre*, by which fhe gained two hundred guineas, and hoped with fuch *Matadores* conftantly at her command to make fome thoufands. But in a fhort time the relations of the young L———

di-

difcovered where they were, and obtain-
ing warrants from a neighbouring Juftice,
releafed them, and commenced an
action againft Mr. N——N.

E 6   CHAP.

C H A P XXIX.

Sequel of the Account of Mrs. N——n's Nunnery. Her Abdication in Wardour-Street. *Purſuits of Mr. N — n. Mrs. N——n enters upon another Nunnery in* Bolton-Street. *Deſcription of her Nuns and Viſitors. Out line of the Characters. A very whimſical, female, hypocritical Character pourtrayed. Some Idea of Mrs. N——n's Male Viſitors, and how perfectly agreeable they might be accommodated, according to their various Diſpoſitions.*

THE rigorous ſteps taken by the relations of Miſs W——ms, in order to bring N——n to juſtice, induced him to decamp, and the noiſe

this

this affair made in the neighbourhood, induced many of the neighbours to pro- pofe indicting the houfe for a diforderly one; and probably if Mrs. N——— had remained much longer upon the fpot, fhe might have mounted the Roftrum, not to *preach*, but to *pray* that the po- pulace would not give her a regale of rotten eggs. Accordingly, a very fhort time after, they both quitted the houfe, and fome time fince we find him in *Gerrard-Street*, keeping what was called a Royal Larder, but in fact a common gaming-houfe, where the Black-Legs of all ranks reforted, from the embroider- ed coat down to the fhirtlefs fharper, with his coat-cuffs pinned tight to pre- vent the difcovery. In this fituation many of them have been taken by the Officers of Juftice, and conveyed to Tothill-fields Bridewell.

AFTER

AFTER fome months had elapfed, when fhe thought the profecution was dropt, Mrs. N——N entered upon another Nunnery, in *Bolton-Street, Piccadilly* Here fhe refolved to play a furer game than in *Wardour-Street:* there fhe had gone too far, rifked too much, and had nearly loft all. At the fame time, fhe refolved to keep up the dignity of her houfe; but then fhe judged it prudent not to foar above profeffed Demireps, or *filles-de-joye* upon the *Haut Ton.*

WE now find among the number of her vifitors, in the latter clafs, Mrs. MARSH—L, Mrs. SM—TH, Mrs. B—KER, Mifs F—SHER, and Mifs H—MET.

THE firft of thefe ladies was the daughter of a parfon, who gave her a genteel education, and endeavoured to fortify

fortify her mind with religion and morality, but upon his death, finding herself in great diftrefs, and being a very agreeable girl, neceffity and importunity prevailed, fhe liftened to the folicitations of Colonel W—n, and refigned her virtue, not her heart, to his intreaties. The Colonel was fucceeded by a man whom fhe fincerely loved, but fhe, too late, found he was pre-engaged in marriage, and after a few weeks amorous dalliance he alfo left her. She was now compelled to roam at large to raife the neceffary fupplies, and occafionally vifits Mrs. W——ston's, Mrs. Nel——n's, and the reft of the Nunneries.

Mrs. Sm—th is a fine genteel woman, though not remarkably beautiful She is very ignorant, and was decoyed by a ftrolling Player, whofe name fhe adopted.

3 To

To avoid ſtarving with him in a Barn, or being ſent to the houſe of correction as a Vagrant (for ſhe too is a Spouter, though

> Her learning only mounts to read a ſong,
> And half the words pronouncing wrong)

ſhe entered the liſt of *Grizettes*; and being introduced to Mrs. N——n as a new face, which ſhe really was in that line of life, has picked up a conſiderable deal of caſh, and now figures away with eclat at Ranelagh, Carliſle-houſe, and the Pantheon.

Mrs. B——ker is a Lady that has till lately been well known upon the Stage; but though ſhe often appeared there characteriſtically a *Goddeſs*, we do not think, when ſhe has quitted the boards, ſhe has any juſt claim to that title. The infidelities of her huſband alſo

upon

upon the Stage, she pleaded as a small excuse for the *lex talionis*, which she had for some time enforced, though not so publickly as she has done within these two years with Count H——G. The Count's finances being some time since much embarrassed, and he having refused to satisfy her pecuniary demands, she now occasionally visits the Nunneries for a temporary admirer, and to procure the *needful*. She also flutters at the Masquerades, and other public places, and when the expansion of her mouth is not seen, she may pass for a good crummy piece.

Miss F—sher has taken upon herself that name, as she fancies she greatly resembles the celebrated Kitty Fisher, who flourished some years since as the most admired Lais upon the *Ton*. That there is some resemblance between them

cannot

cannot be denied; but, in truth, we cannot compliment the prefent Miss F—sher with poffeffing either the perfonal or mental accomplifhments of KITTY; nevertheless fhe is an agreeable girl, and has many admirers amongft perfons of the firft rank.

Miss H——mrt lays claim to a near relationfhip with Mrs LES—ham; but we believe the confanguinity is imaginary. It is certain, that there is fome remote fimilitude of features between them, and fhe imitates that lady as nearly as fhe poffibly can, particularly in her acting, Miss H—met being a great fpouter, and fhe gives out, that fhe fhall be engaged next year at one of the Theatres.

WE cannot clofe the female groupe at Mrs. N—n's, without giving a fketch of a Lady, who unites fafting and falacioufnefs,

ciousnefs, Religion and Vice, in as high
an hypocritic degree as we ever met
with. Mrs. P—— either is, or pretends
to be, the wife of an itinerant Preacher,
some time since immured in the *King's-
Bench.* She is fo extremely devout, that
she confiders it as a deadly fin to put the
leaft morfel of flesh into her *mouth*.—but
we will not fay that she abhors it fo
completely, as never to take a relish of
it in another way, and as abundantly
and voluptuoufly as poffible.—By this
rigid penitence, she has obtained the ap-
pellation of *The Vegetable Syftem*.—Her
devotion is equal to her penance. If she
were to go to bed at five o'clock with
the moft athletic Lover that can be defcribed—and she has no kind of objec-
tion to vigour in a bed fellow—as foon
as she hears the bell for feven o'clock
prayers, she jumps out of bed, huddles
on her clothes, and flies to church or
chapel

chapel to pay her devotions. When thefe are performed, fhe returns to her Enamorato, undreffes, and comes to bed to complete the rites of Venus which fhe had before begun. This, indeed, may be a compendious way of wiping off as fhe goes, which, added to her ſtrict abſtinence from fleſh in one fenfe, or her Vegetable Syſtem, muſt certainly place her in the true and certain high road to Heaven, where there cannot be one turnpike or barrier in her way to impede the progreſs of her celeſtial journey.

WITH fuch beautiful and religious affiftants, Mrs N———N finds means to gratify the taſte and diſpoſition of every kind of cuſtomer. Is he a Philofopher, a Cafuiſt, or a Metaphyfician, Mrs. M——RSHALL can dip into the occult fciences

ences with the moft fubtle logician of
the fchools,—fhe could even hold a converfation, or a difputation, with *Gradus*
himfelf in *Who's the Dupe.* The mere
fenfualift will find ample gratification in
Mrs. Sm—th, as the only ftudy fhe ever
purfued in her life was that of an agreeable Courtezan, and there is not a whim
or caprice that can be fuggefted by the
moft luxuriant imagination of falacious
extravagance, that fhe cannot amply
gratify. Mrs B—ker can *chant* moft
inchantingly, and make you believe her
almoft a goddefs off, as fhe was heretofore
on, the ftage. If pomp and affectation
fhould have any charms in the eye of a
lover, Mifs F—sher can affume all the
coquettifh airs of a firft rate woman of
quality. Should an Enamorato be inclined to hear Desdemona, and many other
capital characterstorturedalmoft to death,
Mifs H—met fmothers her heroine with as
                                        much

much grace as OTHELLO himself. Does the Fanatic Puritan appear moved with the spirit of the flesh, Mrs. P——— will fast and pray with him as long as he pleases—*except in bed*.

No wonder then that Mrs. N———n's male visitors consist of all ranks and denominations, from the spirited Duke who kicks up a riot at the Masquerade (when seconded by a dozen) to shew his valour, down to the meek Methodist field-preacher in *Moorfields*, who fleeces his flock by giving them plenty of *damnation* in the other world, that he may enjoy the sweets and felicities of this mundane sphere in the arms of his Thais.

HAVING, we think, paid due homage at present to Mrs. N———N, we judge it time to renew our visits to our old friends in K——g's-*Place*.

C H A P.

C H A P. XXX.

Present State of the King's Place Nun-
neries. Some original Characters intro-
duced. History of Black HARRIOT;
her first Connexion in Jamaica, *her Ar-*
rival in England, *her eligible Deport-*
ment towards her Master. Emerges in-
to public Life, her Success. Commences
Lady Abbess. The Causes of her Misfor-
tunes, and her present distressed Situa-
tion. Sketches and Anecdotes of the
lovely EMILY, *the bright eyed* PH—Y,
and the pretty COLEB—KL *In which*
are pointed out their first faux pas,
and some broad Hints towards guessing at
their Seducers.

WE shall now return to the great
mart of amour, pleasure, and
bons, the celebrated *sanctum sanctorum* or
King's-

King's-Place. During our late Excur-
fions to *May-Fair* and *Newman-Street*,
there has been a very confiderable revolution in the ftate of affairs at thefe Se-
minaries,—CHARLOTTE HAYES retired
from bufinefs, Mrs. MITCHELL ruined
by her Riding-mafter, an Irifh *jontleman*
of quite independent fortune, and Black
HARRIOT robbed and plundered by
her fervants, and obliged to take refuge
in the King's-Bench: but as we met this
Lady upon the threfhold, tranfferring
what property fhe had to Mrs. DUBE-
RY, we fhall prefently take notice of her
as a very extraordinary character, and as
a proper companion to the *Prince de
Soubife.*

PRESENT *and* EXACT STATE *of the* NUN-NERIES *in* KING's-PLACE, *latitudinally described from the* BEST AUTHORITIES.

Mrs. ADAMS.
Mrs. DUBERY.
Mrs. PENDERGAST.
Mrs. WINDSOR.
Mrs. MATHEWS.

THIS conftellation of Nunneries, which happens to include every houfe in *King's-Place*, fome might think fuffi-cient to fupply the whole polite world with Nuns, and amorous refrefhment; but we know from experience, that nei-ther *Monmouth Street*, though fo long, can produce clothes fufficient for the ten thoufandth part of the inhabitants of this Metropolis, or Whitechapel but-chers meat but for a very fmall part of the inmates of the civic walls.

BEFORE we proceed to enumerate the fair Beauties of thefe Nunneries, we fhall give a little fketch of Black HARRIOT, whilft fhe ftill remains upon this volup tuous fpot She was purchafed amongft other flaves when very young upon the Coaft of Guinea, and carried to Jamaica here fhe was, as ufual, put up to public fale, and purchafed by a capital Planter of Kingfton. As fhe approached near er to maturity, fhe difcovered a lively genius, and a penetration far fuperior to the common run of Europeans, whofe minds had been cultivated by learning. Her mafter now took particular notice of her, and removed her fo far from her late menial capacity, as to make her a fuperintendant of the other female ne-groes. He gave HARRIOT a mafter to teach her to write, read, and fo much of arithmetic as enabled her to keep the do-

meftic

meſtic accounts. He ſoon after diſtin-
guiſhed her ſtill farther from the reſt of
his ſlaves; he being a widower, uſed frequently to admit her to his bed: this
honour was accompanied by preſents,
which ſoon teſtified ſhe was a great favourite In this ſtation ſhe remained for
near three years, during which time
ſhe bore him two children. His buſineſs now calling him to England, HAR-
RIOT accompanied him; and notwith-
ſtanding the Beauties of this Iſland often
attracted his attention, and he frequent-
'y gave a looſe to his natural appetites
with his own country-women, ſtill ſhe
remained unrivalled as a conſtant flame.
Nor was it, in ſome reſpect, extraordinary, for though her complexion might
not be ſo engaging as that of the fair
daughters of Albion, ſhe had many attractions that are not often met with in
the Female World who yield to proſtitu-

tion.

tion. She was faithful to his bed, careful of his domestic concerns, exact in her accounts, and would not suffer any of the other servants to impose upon their master; and in this respect she saved him some hundreds a-year. Her person (to follow her) was very alluring, she was tall, well made, and genteel, and since her arrival in England, she had given her mind to reading, and at her master's recommendation, had perused several useful and entertaining books, calculated for women; whereby she had considerably improved her understanding, and had attained a degree of politeness, scarce to be paralleled in an African female.

SUCH was her situation for many months, but unfortunately her master, or friend, which you please, had

never

never had the small-pox; and having caught it, this malady proved fatal to him, and he paid the great and final mortal tribute upon the occasion. She had made some small provision for herself, with regard to clothes, and some trifling trinkets; but she had acted in so upright and generous a manner towards her departed master, that she had not amassed five pounds in money, though she might easily, and without detection, have been the mistress of hundreds.

THE scene was soon changed, and from being the superintendant of a noble table, she found herself reduced to a scanty pittance, and even that pittance could not last long, if she did not find some means of speedily recruiting her almost exhausted finances.

WE

WE cannot fuppofe that HARRIOT had any of thofe nice, confcientious fcruples, which conftitute what is ufually called Chaftity, and by fome, Virtue. The Daughters of Europe, as well as thofe of Africa, fcarce know their meaning, in their natural ftate, and Nature always directed HARRIOT, notwithftanding fhe had read fome pious, and many moral books. In a word, fhe found it neceffary to make the moft of her jetty charms, and accordingly applied to LOVEJOY to be properly introduced into company. She was quite a new face, in every fenfe of the word, upon the Town, and a perfect phœnomenon of her kind. He difpatched immediately a meffenger to Lord S——, who inftantly quitted the arms of Mifs R——y for this black beauty. The novelty fo ftruck him, with her unexpected improved talents, that he vifited her feveral fucceffive

evenings,

evenings, and never failed giving her at least a twenty pound Bank-note.

SHE now rolled in money, and finding that she had attractions sufficient to draw the commendations and applause of so great a connoisseur in female merit as his Lordship, resolved to vend her charms as dear as possible, and she found that the caprice of mankind was so great, that novelty could command almost any price.

IN the course of a few months she could class in the list of her admirers, at least a score Peers and fifty Commoners, who never presented her with any thing less than soft paper, commonly called a Bank-note. She had ere this realized near a thousand pounds, besides having well stocked herself with clothes, plate, and furniture. One of her friends now ad-

F 4   vised

vifed her to feize a favourable opportunity that prefented itfelf, and fucceed
the late Mrs Johnson in *King's-Place.*
She liftened to this advice, and difburfed
almoft all her little fortune to enter properly upon the premifes.

For fome time fhe had uncommon
fuccefs; but taking a fancy to a certain
Officer of the Guards who had no more
than his pay to fubfift upon, fhe declined accepting the addreffes of any other
admirer; and being at the fame time obliged to dilate frequently her purfe-
ftrings in behalf of this fon of Mars,
fhe foon found a great defalcation in
the ftate of her receipts. Add to this,
fome of her Nuns eloped confidera-
bly in her debt; and being laft feafon
at Brighthelmftone with a party of her
Nuns, the fervants fhe left in charge in
the

the houfe, not only ran her deeply in debt at the fhops in the neighbourhood, but purloined many things of value, which fhe could not recover. She was unwilling to make a legal example of them, though they clofed the fcene of her ruin, and finally conveyed her (tho' indirectly) to the *King's-Bench*, where fhe now remains.

HAVING thus difpatched our black Beauty, let us now look to our fair ones; and to begin with Mrs. ADAMS, at the northern extremity of the conftellation of Nunneries, we there fhall find the lovely EMILY, the bright-eyed PH—Y, and the pretty COLEB—KE.

THIS EMILY is not EMILY C—L-TH—ST, whom we have before defcribed, but EMILY R—BERTS, defcended

from

from a very different family Her father was a very eminent Cutler, *alias* Knife-grinder, and few wheel-barrow artifts had more cuftom than him Neverthelefs, he could not give his EMILY any capital fortune, and fhe was obl'ged to go to fervice She was hired in a creditable tradefman's family, and lived there fome time in an immaculate ftate; but being debauched by her mafter's fon, the fruits of this correfpondence foon became vifible, and fhe was compelled to quit her place. After fhe had given to the World a pledge of her indifcretion, fhe did not find in herfelf much inclination to return to a ftate of fervitude, and the pannel of chaftity being once demolifhed, fhe was eafily perfuaded to think her charms would entitle her to a life of eafe, luxury and diffipation, to which fhe was naturally prone.

prone. It muſt be acknowledged, that EMILY, in the phraſe of *King's Place*, was a very good Piece It is true, ſhe had a ſmall ſcar on one ſide, under her chin; but when ſhe wore a French night cap, it was not viſible, and ſhe was uncommonly agreeable.—Her bro-ther ſtill labours in the humble ſtation of an itinerant Cutler, as ſucceſſor to his fa-ther, but if EMILY has not raiſed him as to dignity, ſhe has improved the emolu-ments of his trade, by having made in-tereſt for him at all the Nunneries of *King's-Place*, and obtained their cuſtom, which is not inconſiderable; and here he almoſt daily labours in his voca-tion.

MISS PH—Y is celebrated for the re-markable brightneſs and vivacity of her eyes; and is, in other reſpects, a genteel, agree-

agreeable girl. She was an apprentice to a Milliner in *Bond-Street*, and was feduced by Lord P——, who foon deferted her, and left her to make the moft of her charms at this general market of Beauty.

Miss Coleb—ke is remarkably pretty, and celebrated for her vivacity and repartee. Mr. R—— the Player had the honour of being the firft upon the lift of her paramours. She was inveigled by an advertifement for an agreeable Figure for the Stage. When fhe had an appointment with him, in confequence of this advertifement, he promifed to teach her the fcenic art, and introduce her to the Acting-Manager, and faid he did not doubt but fhe would prove a great ornament to the Stage, and obtain a handfome falary. He gave her a few dramatic leffons;

fons; but in one of the tender fcenes, he played his part fo well, that fhe was compelled to acknowledge his theatrical powers, and fhe yielded to the directions, and realifed the Poet's moft amorous defcriptions.

CHAP.

C H A P. XXXI.

*An Account of the Nunnery under the Di-
rection of Mrs Dubery. An Outline
of this Lady's Character. Description
of her Visitors. The Diplomatic Body
introduced. A curious Guest in the Person of E—l P—y. A whimsical Platonic Dialogue. Character of this Nobleman. His Incongruities and Absurdities.
A little Touch on the Passions at Lady
P—y's, &c.*

HAVING paid our obeisance to
Mrs Ad—ms, we, in approach-
ing the Equinoctial, sail due south, and
in touching at the next port, necessarily
put into Dubery Bay, where we may
be well victualled, and lay in a proper
store of wine and other liquors, to
enable

enable us to proceed on our voyage through *King's-Place* Streights.

Mrs Dubery is a woman of the World, and though she never read Lord Chesterfield's Letters, can pare her nails, or carve a fowl with as much address and dexterity as his Lordship could himself. Indeed no woman does the honours of the table with more propriety or elegance than herself. She received a boarding-school education; and though her morals might there be a little vitiated by bad examples, and *liaisons indiscrets*, her manners were polished to a degree that would have made her appear a woman of the *Ton*, even in the Drawing room. Vulgarity she utterly abhors, and would as soon subscribe to a bond and judgment, (though she is amazingly fond of her furniture and fixtures) as yield to the impulse of an

aukward

aukward or indelicate word. She has got a fmattering of French, and fpeaks a few words of Italian, by which means fhe can accommodate foreign Noblemen as well as Englifh Senators. The Foreign Minifters, for this reafon, often vifit her Nunnery, and are accommodated to their moft defirable fatisfaction. Count de B——, Monfieur de M——, P—n, Baron de N—, Monfieur de D—, Count de M—, and Count H—, all agree, that the accommodations here are worthy of the Diplomatic Body. In a word, the whole Northern department occafionally vifit her ; and Mrs. DUBERY is not without hopes, and warm hopes, that the Southern department will follow their example.

BUT let it not be imagined, that Mrs. DUBERY's cuftomers confifted entirely of the Members of the Diplomatic Body.

dy. Far was this from the cafe, as we have already hinted; and we have now in our poffeffion an anecdote, that will illuftrate this affertion, we hope, in a pleafing manner. No fooner had E—L P—y returned from America, and paid his refpects in a proper manner at *St. James's* and *Northumberland-Houfe*, than for a while inattentive to his Bill of Divorce, and forgetting his rival Mr. B—D, he repaired to Mrs. DUBERY's, and was by her introduced to LUCY W—LLIAMS, as a girl of beauty, tafte and fentiment; when a dialogue nearly to the following effect took place.

LUCY. My Lord, I flatter myfelf greatly upon this vifit, fo early after your arrival from America; I hope the fatigues of the campaign have been noway prejudicial to your health.

E—L

E—l P—y Not in the least, emulous of distinguishing myself for the good and g'ory of my Country, perils were in this respect a pleasure; and every difficulty I surmounted, gave me fresh vigour, and instead of impairing, improved my health.

Lucy. Your Lordship speaks in the true language of a Hero, and you return at once the Champion of your Country, and the admired Favourite of the Fair Sex, for, as the Poet says, " None " but the brave deserve the fair."

E. P. I find Mrs. Dubery has not deceived me, and that you are the sensible girl she described you. I have the vanity to believe, that I can discriminate the well-bred woman of taste and judgment, though not in the most brilliant

firtu

fituation, from the mere Grizette, who breathes nothing but mere proftitution and contamination. *Vanité apart*, I do confider myfelf as a man of difcernment and fentiment, and th_ugh fometimes, flufhed with libations in public compa-nies by toafting the friends of my Country, I am betrayed into fome irre-gularities, and led into the embraces of incontinent females, 'it is the amiable woman, the fentimental companion that I am at, in affociating with the Fair.

Lucy. I find your Lordfhip is a man of refined tafte and elegant ideas, and rifes far fuperior to the grofs objects of mere fenfation—a gratification which the brute creation enjoy in a far fuperior degree to the rational world, who look upon themfelves as perfect beings, and lords of the univerfe.

E. P.

E. P. Why, I am amazed at the juftnefs and appofitenefs of your reflections! You poffefs the effence of the logic of the Schools, without their lumber; you would do honour to a Profefforfhip!—I could remain with you for an age, but unluckily I have a particular engagement about important bufinefs with Lord GEORGE G——, which obliges me to take my leave fo abruptly.

IN faying this, he put a Bank-note of twenty pounds into her hand, and propofed to renew his vifit the firft opportunity.

No fooner had his Lordfhip retired, than Mrs. DUBERY entered, when LUCY could contain no longer, but burft into a loud fit of laughter; at the fame

time

time difplaying the Bank-note. After having recovered herfelf from this fit of laughter, fhe could not refrain from faying—"This E—l P—y is a more "ridiculous being, if poffible, than "Lord H————n*: He vifits our Se- "minary, in order to have a fentimen- "tal dialogue with a Nun of our fenti- "mental Order, and compliments her "with twenty pounds, to have the plea- "fure and puritanical gratification of "hearing a moral lecture againft fenfu- "ality."

Mrs. Dubery immediately replied in the following manner· "You fur- "prife me greatly!—A girl like you, who "have been upon the Town, and are ac- "quainted with anecdotes and charac-

---

* We fhall have occafion to introduce this ex- traordinary character to our Readers.

"ters

" ters beyond moſt women in your ſpheie,
" that you ſhould be unacquainted with
" P—y's ſtory and infirmities, ſuiprifes
" one wonderfully! The faſt is, that when
' his Lordſhip was at College, he imitat-
" ed many of his fellow collegians, and
" by maſturbation ſo emaciated himſelf,
" as to render him unqualified for the
" duties of matrimony. He neveithe-
" leſs, for the ties of intereſt and fami-
" ly alliance, wedded a moſt beautiful
" young Lady, fraught with all the
" luxuriant taſte of Eaſtern concupiſ-
" cence: for it is ſaid, that ſhe deſcend-
" ed lineally fiom a Sublime Monaich.
" —The World, it is true, is cenforious,
" but I will ſay no more upon that ſub-
" jeſt:—Lady W— M— was certainly
' perfeſtly initiated into all the myſte-
" ries of the Seraglio. To the point.
" Lady P—y was greatly diſappointed.
" —The

" —The nuptial night, and every night
" taught her, that all her conjugal
" hopes and wishes would be frustrated.
" On his part, mortified to the highest
" pitch at his impotent attempts, he
" flew for temporary relief to his pun-
" gent reflexions to wine, and every
" species of debauchery; and in his ine-
" briate frenzy is deluded into an ima-
' ginary opinion, that he is capable of
" receiving that gratification in the
' arms of Proftitution, which the delec-
' table Lady P—y cannot afford him.—
' But the delufion foon ceafes; for tho'
" flattered by his Lais that his powers
' of virility are uncommon, (as truly
" they are) he is confcious, upon the
" flighteft fober reflection, that he is im-
' pofed upon. On the other hand, when
" the intoxicating cup has not operated,
" perfectly confcious of his inability of

" com-

" commanding in the field of Venus,
" however well qualified he may be to
" wield the truncheon in that of Mars,
" he ascribes his impotence to Virtue,
" and assumes the character of another
" Scipio.—But he only makes a virtue
" of necessity; and to avoid exposing
" his incapacity, in attempting a carnal
" connexion, he becomes the Panegy-
" rist of sentimental society with the
" Fair-Sex. Perhaps, in this respect,
" were he to visit all the Nunneries in the
" town, he could not have found a girl
" more capable of pleasing than yourself,
" and therefore, if you play your cards
" properly, you may make your for-
" tune by him alone. Preserve your con-
" stitution, and remain (*sans faire atten-*
" *tion à c'est ce qui s'est passé*) immaculate.
" But I cannot close this miniature,
" without touching upon a feature or
" two which has escaped me. Her La-
                              " dyship

" dyſhip being thus a maiden wife, with
" the falacious blood of the M—s in
her veins, could not reſiſt the impor-
" tunities of Captain F—k—ner of the
" Guards. A fine athletic young man,
" juſt two-and-twenty, renowned for
" his Cyprian atchievements, was an
" object that could not be withſtood.—
" He came, he courted, he conquered.
" This amour was no ſecret; the World
" at large proclaimed it, every Coffee-
" houſe re-echoed with it, and it ſoon
" reached Lord P—y's ears. Mortified to
" the qu..k, and without ſufficient proof
" to eſtabliſh the proof of *Crim. Con.* he
" reſolved to go abroad, and gain ſuch
" military laurels as would cover his
" cornuted brow. He accordingly went
" to America, and there gained honour
" and reputation as a General. The
" death of his mother afforded him a
' ſufficient apology for his return to

" England; efpecially, as he was thereby
" elevated to a feat in the Upper Houfe,
" becoming a Peer in his own right.
" He was now foon poffeffed of fuffi-
" cient vouchers to bring an action for
" *Crim Con* againft Mr. B——D, with
" whom his Lady at prefent cohabited;
" gained a verdict in his favour, and
" is now upon the point of being divor-
" ced by Act of Parliament. But here
" I muft end, as a chair has ftopped at
" the door; and (opening the window-
" fhutters) I fee it is his Excellency
" Monfieur de M— P—N." We fhall
alfo ftop here for a while, and give the
Reader a refpite in point of reading,
that he may relifh the fucceeding Chapter, which will be pretty highly feafon-
ed, with the greater *gufto.*

CHAP.

C H A P. XXXII.

A Trip to Peterfburgh, *by way of Pro-*
logue to the powerful amorous Perform-
ances of Monfieur de M— P—N. *A De-*
fcription of the moft proper Ambaffadors
and Minifters to be fent to that Court,
exemplified in the Perfons of Mr. GUY
D——US, *and Sir* HA—B—Y W——MS.
An Imperial Paffe-partout. *The fala-*
cious Exercifes of two Nymphs in Train-
ing are interrupted by a certain Noble-
man, who engages in performing the Rites
in a Mafculine Manner. Sketch of the
Artifices of an Itinerant Jeweller. Pru-
dence of a celebrated Thais. *Her ju-*
dicious Conduct and Succefs.

IN the frigid clime of *Ruffia*, it would
by fome be thought, that VENUS
there could never have fixed her reign;

G 2   that

that it is incredible she should have quitted her delightful Island of Cyprus, and Paphos, its confecrated capital, to vifit this dreary region but facts are ftubborn things—We find her at *St. Peterfburgh*, with all her blandifhments, in the perfon of the C—A. To quit the figure, in plain Englifh, this Imperial Lady is well known to be one of the greateft Votaries on earth to the Cyprian Goddefs. The officers of her houfhold are all felected from the fineft men in her kingdom, and if report can be credited, fhe has a *paffe-partout**, by which fhe can gain admittance to her dormant Lovers, and feize them in her arms, whilft they teftify their dreaming thoughts by the erected ftandard of fancied blifs; when fhe foon realizes their amorous revenges, and brings them back to their waking fenfes.

---

* A general key that opens all apartments

THE

THE Politicians of Europe are fo well apprized of this Lady's uncontroulable paffion for amorous delight, that there is not a Court who is in friendfhip with her, but what confults more the comelinefs and athletic appearance of the Ambaffadors and Minifters they appoint for *Peterfburgh*, than their political abilities. To negociate there with fuccefs, an Envoy muft have ftudied *Aretin* more than *Machiavel* Did the pride and infolence of the Grand Signior permit him to fend Ambaffadors to Foreign Courts, and had he appointed a Bafh w with *Three Tails* for *Ruffia*, moft probably there never would have been a rupture between him and the C—a. The mifunderftanding between the E——s and *France*, previous to the laft war, was entirely owing to the French Ambaffador at *Peterfburgh* being an emaciated Macaroni, and we may attribute the good underftanding

that

that has so long subsisted between us and *Russia*, to the powers and abilities of Mr Guy D—k—us and Sir Hanbury W—ms; and we hope, for the honour and advantage of this country, that Sir James H— will not fall short, in giving her Imperial M—y similar and equally convincing proofs, how much he has the gratification of the Cz——a's most fervent wishes deeply at heart. As a testimony of her Majesty's sensibility of this Gentleman's merit and abilities, we shall only quote her feeling expressions on conferring the honour of Knighthood upon him.

When she invested him with the Order of the Bath, the ceremony concluded as follows: " Then taking from a " table a gold-hilted sword richly orna- " mented with diamonds, the Empress " touched his left shoulder three times " with

" with it, pronouncing thefe words,
" *Soyez bon et honorable Chevalier, au*
" *Nom de Dieu.* (Be a good and ho-
" nourable Knight, in God's name.) And
" on his rifing up and *kiffing* her Impe-
" rial Majefty's hand, the Emprefs
" added, *Et pour vous prouver combien*
" *je fuis* CONTENTE', *de vous, je vous fais*
" *prefent de l'Epée avec laquelle je vous*
" *ai fait Chevalier* (And to convince you
" how well CONTENTED I am with you,
" I make you a prefent of the Sword
" with which I knighted you)."

THE following anecdote of M. DE
M— P—, which may be depended upon,
will eafily account for this gentleman's
being fo great a favourite of the E.——fs,
as to be appointed her M——r at this
Court.

AT the conclufion of the laft Chapter,
we had fet down Monfieur de M— P—'s
chair

chair at Mrs. DUBERY's, where we left
the Chairmen and the Reader to breathe
a little after their fatigue—We now
think it time to attend this gentleman
into the parlour, where he is introduced
by that Lady to LAURA C——NS and
SOPHIA L——CE, two young Tits just
broke in by the judicious Mrs DUBERY
This gentleman's powers had been very
well established in the purlieus of St
James's, and Lady H————N had dig-
nified him with the title of *Son Excell-
lence à Quatorze*. Upon the present occasion he supported the same character;
—for having retired to bed with LAURA
and SOPHY, they found, in the course
of an hour and a half, that they were
uncommonly fatigued, having each un-
dergone seven different attacks, without
his Excellency being in the least out of
breath; and he retired with the greatest
sang froid, still capable of half a dozen
fresh

frefh onfets, if the opportunity fhould prefent itfelf.

AFTER he was dreffed, he gave each of his Nymphs five guineas, telling them, that they were totally ignorant of their profeffion, and that he fhould, before the end of the week, give them another leffon. The fact was, that in the courfe of thefe amorous evolutions he had called into play moft of *Aretin's* poftures, and, to fpeak in a maritime phrafe now fo much in vogue, they had never been ufed to any other than *plain failing* They accordingly promifed to perfect themfelves in thefe exercifes againft the next time his Excellency came.

ACCORDINGLY, the following day they ftript quite naked in the *Salon d'Amour,* and went through every evolution of

G 5

Aretin, having this great *Attitudina-*
rian's work before them.—they had already compleated the firft rehearfal, and
were now in the *Bafket-fly*, when Lord
DEL—AINE entered, and was fo fmitten
with their charms, that he defired the
reprefentation fhould be more charafter-
iftic and natural, and requefted to perform the man's part; and confidering
this was his firft effay, and that his
Lordfhip had been up all night at the
Hazard table, where he had loft his laft
guinea, a circumftance fuffic ent to difpirit
any man, he went through the different
evolutions and exercifes with uncommon
dexterity. Mrs. DUBERY knew that his
Lordfhip was a perfect man of honour
with regard to gaming-debts, and h s
amorous engagements; and therefore,
at his requeft, gave the *Pupils of Nature*
a couple of guineas each, for the pleafure,

fure, amufement, and gratification he had received.

His Lordfhip foon after departed, to go home to drefs, and recruit his finances, by the help of an ufurious Son of Levi. No fooner had his Lordfhip taken his leave, than another Son of Levi made his appearance. This was no other than the itinerant Jeweller, Mr. L—z—rus, who waited upon the La-dies to receive their orders; or, in other words, to difpofe of as much of his cargo as he could perfuade them to pur-chafe. By this traffic, Mr. L——s has amaffed a very pretty fortune, and ftill continues raifing annually a very confi-derable fum, by the profits (not fmall) of vending baubles and trinkets to the ignorant girls-at the different Nunneries about Town, and to Women in Keep-ing, who, by profiting of the opportu-

nity

nity of his appearing whilft their keepers are prefent, *fall in love* fometimes with half his cafket, when their generous friends feldom refufe the importunities of the fair Advocates for thefe alluring ofnaments. At other times, knowing their connections, he will give them credit to almoft any amount, as far as he thinks them able to pay; but upon the fmalleft failure of their promife, Mr. LATITAT makes his appearance, and foon reminds them there is a legal method of recovering the debt. This peregrinating Jeweller is faid to be one of the beft cuftomers to the practitioners of the Law, of any trader within the Bills of Mortality he keeps one Attorney in conftant practice, who lives genteelly, and keeps his girl and his phaeton with the emoluments arifing from Mr. L—z—s's cuftom. He eafily perfuaded LAURA to lay out all her gains of the

two

two laft days—the prefent of his *Excellence à Quatorze*, and that of Lord DEL.—NE, in a pair of pafte-buckles, and a pair of ear-rings of the fame manufacture; but having occafion for cafh a fhort time after, fhe could raife no more upon them at her Uncle's than half-a-guinea. SOPHY was more prudent, and as fhe had fome expectations of being taken into keeping, and paffing for a married woman, fhe purchafed nothing but a plain gold ring, which, however, fhe paid pretty handfomely for.

LUCY, who had more difcretion than either of thefe young *Tits*, gave them, after the Jew's departure, a pretty fevere lecture upon their folly and extravagance, and told them, as afterwards appeared, that they had paid more than double the value of what they had purchafed.

chafed. As to her part, fo far from fquandering her money in that ridiculous manner, fhe had realized a pretty confiderable fum, with which fhe propofed foon to take a houfe, and commence Lady Abbefs herfelf. To this end, as the money fhe had faved was fcarcely fufficient to accomplifh her defign, fhe refolved to make a certain friend of Earl P—y; and it was alfo requifite, for fear of jealoufy or revenge for quitting the houfe of Mrs. DUBERY, and fetting up in oppofition to her, to fettle their accounts previoufly in an amicable way; which fhe fpeedily did, and having obtained a genteel releafe in writing, thereby became entirely out of her clutches.

Upon Earl P——y's next vifit, fhe took uncommon pains to ingratiate herfelf in his favour; and as he was rather

ther elevated with liquor, and, as ufual
in that fituation, falacioufly inclined,
fhe called to her aid fuch meretricious
arts, as gave him, even in his debilitated ftate, fuch raptures as he never before had been acquainted with. He
fwore fhe was the only woman that
knew perfectly how to pleafe; and that
he fhould never think of any other female, if fhe would promife to be conftant to him. Nothing could be more
happily opportune to her moft fanguine
wifhes: Lucy told him, fhe had it in
contemplation for fome time, to quit
the way of life fhe was then in, and
confine herfelf entirely to the embraces
of one man; and that his Lordfhip was
the perfect object of her wifhes and her
ambition · that fhe propofed taking
a genteel houfe, and furnifhing it in a
proper manner; but that unfortunately
fhe was deficient in cafh:—" If (fhe
" added)

" added) she could so far trespass upon
" his Lordship's generosity, as to re-
" quest the loan of a small sum for a
" few months, she doubted not but she
" should be able, at the expiration of
" that time, to repay him with interest,
" if he required it."—His Lordship
stopt her before she proceeded any farther, and calling for pen and ink, gave
her a draft upon his Banker for five
hundred pounds.

THIS capital stroke being struck,
Lucy's thoughts were solely-engaged in
seeking for a house in a proper situation,
and furnishing it in a frugal, but elegant manner. She hit upon one in the
environs of *Brook Street, Grosvenor-
Square*, and attended most of the genteel
auctions, to purchase, if possible, such
furniture as she wanted at a cheaper
rate than at the shops.

Lucy's

Lucy's defign was foon difcovered by Mrs. Dubery, not only by her frequent abfence from home, but by her refufing to go into the company of any gentleman except Earl P——y, who frequently called upon her to chat away half an hour, and enquire concerning her welfare, and the progrefs of her new plan of operations. Mrs Dubery was greatly mortified to think fhe had been the indirect caufe of alienating fo good a cuftomer (which certainly would be the cafe) as Earl P—y, and probably many more. However, fhe prudently checked her refentment, and pretended great friendfhip towards Lucy;—faying, as her plan was now no fecret, fhe begged that a perfect cordiality might fubfift between them ; and that by playing into one another's hands, they might fecure the greateft part, if not the whole genteel and valuable trade to themfelves.

Lucy

LUCY was glad to find that Mrs. DU-BERY put matters upon this amicable footing, and she readily acquiefced in what this Lady propofed. We fhall foon have an opportunity of vifiting LUCY in her new habitation; in the mean while we think the following ge-nuine *Hiftoriette* will not be difagreeable to our Readers.

CHAP.

C H A P. XXXIII.

Historiette, or, Memoirs of Lord DEL——NE; *being the Outline of his Amours, Marriage, and Pursuits, for the last Twenty Years. His Gallantries, Revels, and juvenile Dissipations. His Connexion with the celebrated Miss* HERMITAGE. *A whimsical Intrigue, and its more whimsical Consequences, in the Persons of Mr. and Mrs.* CHATEAUR——Y. *His Acquaintance with Miss* H——LLAND. *His Distresses. Marries Mrs.* KN——GHT, *to repair his Fortune. His Behaviour to her. A curious Billet. Miss* HOLL——ND's *Elopement. Recovers her. His Wife's Retreat to a Convent;——and his Lordship's present Indigence and Pursuits.*

SO very conspicuous a character as Lord DEL——NE, who has figured upon the horizon of gaiety and dissipa-

tion

tion for upwards of twenty years, muſt certainly afford a variety of ſituations, pleaſant, intereſting, whimſical, capricious, and riſible. We therefore thought, introducing him to our Readers *propriâ perſonâ*, would afford them ſome variety, and produce an agreeable digreſſion in theſe Memoirs. After this ſhort preface, we ſhall deſcribe his perſon, character, and diſpoſition.

Lord D—L—NE is deſcended from a noble and illuſtrious family in *Scotland*, and was next heir to a Ducal Coronet, which induced many Ladies of the firſt rank and fortune to look at him with a partial and a wiſhful eye, as a mate for life His perſon was, beſides, genteel and handſome, which his taſte for dreſs ſet off to the greateſt advantage. But he was reſolved, as long as he could conveniently, to enjoy his freedom; and.

at

at a very juvenile period of life, roamed
at large amongst all the come-at able
Beauties and Demireps within the Bills of
Mortality. Thefe, added to the expences
conftantly attendant upon intrigue, a
ftrong propenfity to extravagance, and
an infurmountable itch for play, foon
diftreffed him, and he found his fortune
out at the elbows almoft as foon as he
had got poffeffion of it. The firft re-
markable Thais we find upon the lift of
his Enamoratas was the celebrated Mifs
HERMITAGE, with whom he kept up a
correfpondence for feveral months; but
her luxuriant difpofition and extravagance compelled him to break off this
connection; and fhe found a fucceffor
in the perfon of the Tripoline Ambaffador, who had eftablifhed his character
for his amorous abilities as well as his
generofity, and with whom fhe lived during the remainder of his refidence at this

I   Court,

Court, in a brilliant and fuperb manner.

The next confpicuous connection of Lord Del—ne was Mrs. Chateaur—y, who had not long celebrated her nuptials with a French Linguift; but her *Caro Spofo*, ere the honey-moon had elapfed, treated her with fuch indifference—frequently leaving her without the common neceffaries of life, that fhe refolved to difpofe of her charms to the beft bidder, and live with eafe and comfort. She had fcarce come to this pious refolution, before a Duenna of fome fkill in negociations of this kind introduced her to Lord Del—ne, and he took her home to his houfe in *Conduit-Street*. The little Language-Mafter was very well pleafed to get rid of his wife, as he might probably get a handfome fum by a profecution for *crim. con* But his Lordfhip receiving intimations

of

of his defign, made overtures to Mr.
CH——Y, to compromife the matter;
and a negociation was fet on foot, which
foon terminated in an agreement on the
part of the hufband to give up all pretenfions to his wife, and drop the profecution, on condition of receiving the
fum of two hundred pounds. Thefe preliminaries being fettled, his Lordfhip
met him at a Tavern near *Soho* to pay
him the money, which he accordingly
did. They dined together; and after
drinking a bottle, his Lordfhip propofed a party at piquet. The Linguift
plumed himfelf much upon his fkill at
this game, and very readily accepted the
challenge. But the Blind Goddefs did
not vouchfafe to befriend him; and tho'
a cuckold, he had fuch ill-luck, as to
difpofe of his wife, and lofe every guinea of her purchafe-money in a few
hours.

hours. Upon his Lordship's return to his Dulcinea, after a hearty laugh, he told her, that he had settled matters with her husband in every sense of the word, and pulling out the cash, flung it into her lap, saying, " There is the value " of you !—but see if you cannot make " a better use of it than your foolish hus- " band."

NOTWITHSTANDING this purchase made in form, he did not long remain in possession of the premises, and the cause of his Lordship's quitting the Tenement, or rather ejecting the Tenant, was truly laughable, though strictly true.—Mrs. CH——y and the Duenna, who then lived together, were entertaining a gentleman who dined with them (in expectation of meeting his Lordship concerning some business), with the follies, foibles, and caprices

of

of his Lordſhip. Mrs. CH——Y went
ſo far as to reveal the myſteries of the
interior Cyprian Temple, and commu-
nicate ſome anecdotes of his having re-
courſe to *Cantharides* as well as *Birch* ;
and in order to corroborate her aſſer-
tions, as the gentleman ſeemed to give
little credit to them, but looked upon
them as the mere effuſions of joviality,
ſhe added, " Why, Sir, you may
" think his Lordſhip is a ſtout man, to
" view his well-ſhaped leg, but here,
" Sir (going to a drawer, and produ-
" cing a ſtocking with a falſe quilted
" calf), it is to this device he owes the
" ſymmetry and athletic appearance of his
" leg." The gentleman was aſtoniſhed
at what he had ſeen, and could not refrain from joining in the laugh: however, he never revealed the ſecret with
which he was thus entruſted to his

Lordſhip, but D—NE's Valet having a
particular pique againſt the Duenna, and
willing to rout the party, in order to re-
gain his Lordſhip's confidence, and
fleece him, as heretofore, entirely himſelf, no ſooner opened him the door,
upon his return home in the evening,
than, following him into the parlour,
he revealed to him all that had paſſed in
his abſence, with ſome aggravating cir-
cumſtances, which ſo enraged his Lordſhip, that, to avoid the arms of Mrs.
CHATEAU——Y, who was then in bed,
he repaired to a Bagnio, and ſent for the
firſt girl the waiter recommended, leaving a letter, or reſcript, intimating that he
could diſpenſe with Mrs CHATEAU—Y's,
as well as the Duenna, Mrs. DUS—INS's,
abſence. In conſequence of this warning, they found it expedient to retire
the next morning before breakfaſt, as the
Valet had received poſitive orders never

to

to let them eat or drink again in the houfe.

SCARCE had Mrs. CHATEAU—Y and Mrs. DUSS———NS decamped, before he brought home Mifs HOLL—ND. That famous or infamous antiquated Beldame Lady GUNST——N was, we are well informed, the negociator upon this occafion. This young Lady was the daughter of a Peruke-maker, near *Red Lion-Square, Holborn.* She was remarkably handfome and genteel, and not above nineteen. She was originally feduced by Lady GUNST——N, who now affured her that Lord DEL———NE had protefted to her in the moft folemn manner, he propofed marrying her; but that he could take no fuch ftep till the demife of a near relation, whom he was in fome meafure dependent upon, and therefore was very cautious not to dif-

pleaf

pleafe him;—but that fhe would certainly not only be a Peerefs, but alfo a Duchefs, in all probability, if fhe did not, by rejecting his prefent propofal, run counter to her own intereft. The idea of a Ducal Coronet was irrefiftible; and fhe yielded to the infinuations of Lady G——n and his Lordfhip's importunities.

Miss H——d had not long engaged in this alliance, before his Lordfhip's affairs became in a very diftracted ftate, and he had no other probable refource but marriage. His rank and expectations had long fince enabled him to marry a woman of fortune, but the word *Marriage* had always terrified him, and he had hitherto preferred freedom to affluence. But now diftrefs and penury ftared him in the face—his credit was entirely exhaufted, and all his refources were

dried

dried up : in a word, neceffity prevailed
upon him to purfue this rafh ftep ; and
he foon found means to ingratiate himfelf with Mrs. Kn—ght, a Widow-La-
dy of very confiderable fortune. Ambition was her motive—want and mifery
his excitements Then hands were joined, but their hearts remained dif-united ;
and what is pofitively fact, he never
bedded with her but one night; and
having in the morning gained poffeffion
of all that fhe could difpofe of, about
noon he took a French leave, and never
afterwards vifited her He wrote her a
laconic billet nearly in the following
terms.

" My Lady,

" YOU muft be confcious that Na-
" ture has been fo unkind to you, as to
" have denied you the powers of pro-

pagating

" pagating your fpecies. Therefore,
" Madam, it were in vain for me to
" tantalize myfelf and your Ladyfhip,
" to obtain what neither you can grant,
" nor I can obtain. My beft wifhes,
" however, attend you, and in grati-
" tude for the kindnefs I have received
" at your hands, fhall ever confider my-
" felf as

        " Your much obliged

                " Friend and Hufband,

                        " DEL——NE."

THE Reader will probably be dubious,
whether this charge was well grounded,
or whether the defect he complains of
might not be on his fide. All we can
venture to decide upon this occafion is,
that Mrs. KN—GHT never bore her firft
hufband any children, though it is well
known he had been the father of feveral

                                    by

by other women We shall leave this matter to the Reader's own judgment and determination, to proceed to the sequel of this Historiette, which has rather swelled upon our hands, and which we shall therefore wish to curtail as much as possible.

UPON Lord DEI—NE's marriage being proclaimed in the papers, Miss HOL-I—D, who was not made acquainted with the design, took the alarm, and irritated to the highest degree that all her hopes had now vanished of being Lady DEL——NE, before his return on the day after his nuptials, she had quitted his house, and taken with her all her clothes, in a coach, leaving behind her this short Card.

" PERFIDIOUS Man!—I leave
" you to the remorse of your own con-
H 4   " science,

" fcience, for the injuries you have done
" me. and as to that vile wretch Lady
" G——n, if there be juftice on Earth
" or in Heaven, the wrath of that Di-
" vine Power who fuperintends the deeds
" of this Nether Ball, muft be hurled
" upon her.

   " Adieu for ever,

    " The moft injured of her Sex."

Upon the receipt of this billet, he
was almoft diftracted. He pofted to
every part of the Town in fearch of his
dear Holl——nd, but all his purfuits
were ineffectual that day. On the mor-
row, his fervant recognizing the coach-
man who had taken her up, on his ftand,
traced her to an obfcure lodging near the
Minories, where an aunt of her lived,
and kept a green-fhop. His Lordfhip
foon haftened thither, and failed not to
ufe all the rhetoric he was mafter of to

       perfuade

perfuade her to return to *Conduit-Street.*
He pleaded his diftrefs ;—he fhewed her
the letter he had wrote to his wife ; and
affured her of his inviolable conftancy
and fidelity to the only female he efteemed on earth, who was Mifs HOLL—ND.
This logic, with the ftill more perfuafive
eloquence of a thoufand pound Bank-
note, had its influence, and fhe returned home with him.

Now his Lordfhip was at the higheft
pinnacle of mundane felicity——in poffeffion of the charmer of his foul—roll-
ing in money—bidding defiance to his
creditors, after exorcifing two bailiff's
followers, who were in poffeffion of his
demefnes. He revelled at large in luxury
and diffipation, thofe two idols of his
inceffant devotion.

H 5   As

As to Lady DEL—NE,—having by her generosity to her husband reduced herself to a very scanty pittance, she found it expedient to retire to a Convent in *Flanders*, where she some time since ended her days; which, probably, were shortened by reflecting upon her folly, and the mortification of having sacrificed every thing that was dear to her, for the empty whistling of a title.

His Lordship failed not to testify his taste for gaiety, and every kind of fashionable extravagance, whereby he soon got rid of all Mrs. KN—GHT's fortune; and has been for a considerable time reduced to the necessity of his wits, or rather the folly of others, for a maintenance. We shall terminate this Chapter with a sentence from La Fontaine, but

but to whom applicable we will not pretend to say:

" *On commence par être Dupe, et l'on*
" *finit par être Fripon.*

CHAP.

C H A P XXXIV.

A Visit to the celebrated Mrs W—rs. Description of her Rout. Account of her Company. Some unexpected Visitors. Colonel B—den's Anecdotes upon the Occasion. The Rival Daughter. The Amorous Mother. The Conflict, or critical Scene, in which a celebrated Singer is a principal Actor. The favourable Prospect of succeeding in his Address. A satyrical Picture of the Metempsychosis, or the Transmigration of the Souls of Lady H—, Lady P—, the Marchioness of C—, Lady G—, Miss H—, and Mrs. J—, by Lord P———.

BEFORE we pay a visit in form to Mrs PENDERGAST, who is, according to succession, our next neighbour in *King's-Place*, we cannot refuse

an

an invitation we have received to wait upon the celebrated Mrs. W——rs, a Lady entirely upon the *Haut Ton*, who keeps a houfe of rendezvous for *Demireps* and *Beaux Garçons* of the fuperior clafs, and who is alfo a profeffed matchmaker, and has by thefe honourable and induftrious purfuits rolled a genteel equipage, and fupported a houfehold, confifting of fervants of almoft every denomination.

HERE we found Beaux and Belles, Wits and Wags, Muficians and Singers. The group at our firft entrance confifted of Lord P——y, Colonel Bo—DEN, Mr. A——NS——D, and Mr. C—B—D. The Ladies were Lady II—N, Lady P—Y, the Marchionefs of C——N, Lady GR——R, and Mrs. J—s. Several other vifitors, male and female, foon after appeared. In fuch a refpecta-ble

ble company, we flattered ourfelves with the moft exalted entertainment, as Wit and Beauty here triumphantly reigned. But as ufual in mixed companies, where play is *almoft* the predominant paffion, two card-tables were filled, and Spadille and Bafto were the *paffe-paroles*. However, occafionally, a little flander would diffufe itfelf. "Pray," faid Lady H— to Lady P—y, in half a whifper that was heard by all the room, " have you " heard any thing of the affair of " Lady J— and Mr. W—n?" " Who " is this W—n ?" faid the Marchionefs, " I cannot learn. There was an Offi- " cer, feemingly of a Marching Regi- " ment, who ufed to go backwards and " forwards, when his Lordfhip was out " of town—I'll be whipt if it is not him. " —*The Red Aces, if you pleafe, Lady* " *H—n?*—" *Oh! my Lady,*" replied Lady

Lady H——n, "*I am certain I had Pon-*"*to.*" "*That can't be,*" replied the Marchioneſs; "*here it is in my hand.*"—After this altercation, which had like to have become pretty warm, ſubſided—Lady L–r inquired what ſort of a man this Officer was. To this the Marchioneſs replied, " She had never ſeen his face, but " that, by his back and legs, he was a " ſtout, athletic perſon." " Oh!" reſumed Lady L–r, " I never mind a " man's face, provided he has got a noſe " on it : and the longer the better; it is " a pretty ſure *index*, if he is ſtout and well- " made."

THE converſation had got thus far, when Miſs H—x was announced. Several of the company were aſtoniſhed, to ſee ſo much apparent innocence ſeated in the countenance of any young lady, ſcarce nineteen, intitled to a very ample fortune,

in

in fuch a Female Coterie; but this furprize was carried ftill farther upon the
introduction of Mr. L—NI the Singer,
accompanied by another Mufician.

COLONEL BOW——EN now took us
afide, and acquainted us, but not without a tolerable, or rather intolerable
fhare of ftuttering and ftammering,
" That L——I, being introduced to
" Mrs. D——N, the young Lady's mo-
" ther, on account of the finenefs of his
" trills, this Lady, who was very fond
" of mufic, particularly where it was
" fuftained in a manly manner, was fo
" ravifhed at this Son of LEVI's finging,
" that in defpite of any little lofs he
" might have fuftained by circumcifion,
" fhe was urged to make fuch overtures
" as he could not poffibly mifunder-
" ftand, and that fhe had the vanity
" to think her perfonal charms and
" the

" the fortune she possessed, which was so
" ample, (not forgetting her Pension
" upon the Irish Establishment) were
" sufficient to captivate a vagrant, who
" had no other hope or expectation than
" a *quaver* for his support, and which
" might fail him, as it had done many
" other Singers of superior eminence
" (meaning herself amongst that num-
" ber), notwithstanding she was now
" verging upon fifty. But as she
" thought this was a profound secret to
" every one but her confidante, she had
" judiciously put herself down at forty,
" where she had stuck for upwards of
" nine years."

THE Colonel having got through this
sentence with some difficulty, he paused
a little, and then proceeded. " Now, if
" we may credit report, there has already
" been a little *blendation* of Christian and
" Jewish

" Jewish flesh, for it is whispered, that
" upon her confidante's reproving her
" indiscreet conduct, she grew nettled,
" and could not refrain uttering in a
" very loud tone of voice, that was over-
" heard by the servants—*Why, you old*
" *fool, don't you know I am above scandal?*
" *—Besides, what risk do I run? An't I,*
" *though I don't chuse to let the World*
" *know it, past child-bearing? I was re-*
" *solved to look before I leaped! I did not*
" *chuse to buy a pig in a poke! I was re-*
" *solved to know my man, before I engaged*
" *for life!* Having said this, she
" bounced out of the room, and repair-
" ing unexpectedly to her Daughter's
" dressing apartment, discovered her
" reading a letter; which exciting her jea-
" lousy, and thinking she recollected the
" hand, she was induced abruptly to
" snatch it out of her Daughter's hand,
" and upon perusing it, found it, as she
" judged,

" judged, written by L—r, and containing
" the moft tender and paffionate decla-
" rations, with fome oblique hints that
" her mother's paffion for him, which
" was too vifible for any one not to ob-
" ferve, was quite fulfome and difguft-
" ing to him.

" ENRAGED at this difcovery, fhe tore
" the letter to pieces, upbraided her
' Daughter in the moft violent manner,
' and was upon the point of ordering
" her chair, to call upon the infolent
" faithlefs *chanter* (not *inchanter* upon
' this occafion), but before fhe had
" huddled on her clothes, the unfortu-
" nate Enamorato knocked at the door.
" He was, as ufual, ufhered in , when he
" had a fcene to go through, that, not-
" withftanding his *uncommon* modefty,
" put him to the blufh, and greatly dif-
" concerted him. No fooner did the
" ftorm

" storm begin, than he was for making
" a precipitate retreat ; but this was pre-
" vented by the door being locked upon
" him. The charge was now brought
" home to him, and he was compelled
" to collect a sufficient share of decent
" assurance to deny being the writer of
" the letter, which luckily for him was
" destroyed. His bold asseverations, or
" rather her vanity, induced her to give
" some credit to what he asserted , and
" she being now somewhat appeased,
" after having hummed her one way, he
" now hummed her another, in humming
" a favourite air, in which he vowed and
" protested, by all the Gods and Goddes-
" ses, the sincerity of his passion for her.
" The scene now changed ; and if, from
" their silence, and the cracking of the
" sopha, any thing could be surmised
" as to their present situation, the pas-
" sion of rage was soon converted into
" that of love.

Thoug'

" THOUGH L—I's ready and pofitive
" affurances had delivered him from his
" unexpected and violent embairaffment,
" he was fearful of rifking again fuch a
" fituation; and has therefoie, fiom that
" hour, never paffed the threfhold of
" Mrs. D—N's dooi. His abfence foon
" convinced her, that fhe had been de-
" ceived and deluded by his mellifluous
" tongue. She could not now refrain
" coming to an open iuptuie with her
" Daughter, who, unable to bear the re-
" fentment and jealoufy of hei Mother,
" quitted the houfe, and has taken refuge
" under the aufpices of our refpectable
" hoftefs. His arrival at this juncture
" plainly indicates that matters are going
" on fwimmingly, through the mediation
" of Mrs. W—T—RS; and I doubt not
" but a fhort time will convince the
" World, that they are united in wedlock,
" notwithftanding all the endeavours of

" her Mother, and her application to
" Chancery, to prevent it."

Mr. L—l was now requested to sing
a song, which he readily complied with,
and was accompanied by his friend upon the German flute; after which they
both received general applause.

Lord P—f—t having selected our
little circle from the rest of the company, could not refrain giving vent to his
sarcastic vein. Said his Lordship, " I
" am a disciple of Pythagoras, and firm-
" ly believe in a Metempsychosis
" Whilst L—l was singing, I was ru-
" minating what would be the most pro-
" bable transmigration of the souls of
" the Ladies present I could not help
" thinking, that Lady H—'s would
" take up her abode in a Goat of the
" most vicious kind. Lady P—l's
" would

" would perhaps animate a Wagtail.
" The Marchionefs of C——n's might
" wriggle her tail in the figure of a proud
" B—h. Lady Gr——'s would cer-
' tainly occupy the fmall, but falacious
" body of a Frog, as this animal is faid to
" be the longeft in the act of coition of
" any living creature. Poor H——x,
" whom I heartily pity, her foul would
" certainly take refuge in an innocent
" Lamb, doomed a victim. and as to
" Mrs. J—, I think nothing would fuit
" her but a Viper, a Toad, or a Rattle-
" fnake." His Lordfhip having gone
thus far in giving a fcope to his imagination, upon the tranfmigration of the
Ladies fouls, he was interrupted by a
favourite air from Mr. L—i, to which
every one paid the moft earneft attention, and for which he again received
the repeated plaudits of the company.

CHAP.

CHAP. *XXXV.

*An Outline of the Character of Mrs.
Br—dshaw. A Description of her Visitors of both Sexes. An Audience with
some of the Diplomatic Body of the Southern Department. Some Female Puns,
rather unexpected. Lord Champetre
introduced. Sketch of Lady Champetre, with some Account of her
Amours, and their Consequences.*

NOW we are upon our emigrating
tour from *King's-Place*, we will
pay a friendly visit to an old acquaintance in *Queen-Anne's-Street*. It should
seem that we were somewhat remiss in
our first Edition, in having overlooked
a rendezvous of such eminence as that of
Mrs. Br—dshaw, but to acknowledge
the fact, we were, at the time of these

Volumes firſt going to preſs, unacquainted with the ſubſequent anecdotes, at
leaſt in part.

WE will not pretend to trace, with a
biographic exactitude, the genealogy of
Miſs FANNY HERBERT, we ſhall, therefore, *pick her up*, as we firſt found her, in
Bow-Street. Soon after this period ſhe
commenced buſineſs for herſelf, and
kept a very *reputable Brothel*, the corner
of the Play-houſe paſſage, in the ſame
ſtreet.

" Here long ſhe *flouriſhed*,
" —— Sweet to ſenſe, and lovely to the eye!"

SHE was a fine ſhewy woman; tall
and elegant, of a fair complexion, with
good eyes, remarkably regular white
teeth, and we believe had as little re-
courſe to the coſmetic art as any nymph

of the Garden. Her houfe was elegantly furnifhed; a good fide-board of plate caught the vifitor's eye, and her nymphs in general were tolerable good Pieces. A rich Cit was her moft frequent companion, and probably chief fupport, but though fhe was not lavifh of her favours, fhe was not invincible to the perfuafive rhetoric of a fine young fellow of two-and twenty, with broad fhoulders, and well timbered. Captain H—, Mr B——, Mr. W—, and feveral more who came up to her *ftandard*, weie occafionally admitted to her embraces; but it muft be acknowledged, that fhe was far from being mercenary; and thefe gentlemen, who were all *beaux garçons de profeffion*, fo far from increafing her revenues, rather diminifhed them, as they were for the moft part upon the Sinking Fund eftablifhment.

At

At length she met with a gentleman of confiderable fortune who was infatuated with her charms, and fo defirous of having her folely to himfelf, (which he thought could no other way be compaf-fed than by marriage) that he abfolute-ly offered her his hand in an *honourable* way, and to convince her he was per-fectly ferious in this propofal, he took a genteel houfe in *Queen-Anne's-Street* (where fhe now refides)—furnifhed it for her in an elegant manner, and fixed the day of their intended nuptials, but being fuddenly taken ill, he was advi-fed by his phyficians to repair to *Bath* for the recovery of his health—and here he paid the great debt of Nature before the celebration of their nuptials. Hav-ing affumed his name upon her firft ap-pearance in *Queen-Anne's-Street*, fhe has ever fince retained it.

FINDING

FINDING herself in this unexpected dilemma, she for some time knew not what course to steer, and not having entirely quitted her house in *Bow-Street*, still continued it on, in the old train of variegated prostitution; but having soon after got into a more polite track, she discontinued her house in *Covent Garden*, and retired totally to *Queen-Anne's-Street*.

HER house now became one of the most polished receptacles for elegant intrigue, as no woman can, when she pleases, comport herself with more propriety than FANNY; she has also a pretty fluency of small-talk, and occasionally throws in a pleasant *equivoque:* in this respect she may be pronounced the second edition of LUCY COOPER. Indeed FANNY imitates her too much, and sometimes unsuccessfully; but upon the
whole,

whole, she is a vivacious, agreeable companion, and, though in the wane of life, still a desirable Piece.

AT her house occasionally may be met with the agreeable Miss M——n, the frolicksome Mrs W——n, and the lively Miss T——h These Ladies alternately frequent *King's-Place* and the other Nunneries, but are never so much at home to their mind as in *Queen-Anne's-Street.*

THE first of these Ladies is much admired by the Chevalier P——o, the Portugueze M——r Mrs W——n, either out of jealousy or whim, calls him M——n's *Pintle* The Chevalier overheard this one evening, as he was getting out of his chair, and was not a little nettled at the *pun*, till FANNY assured him it was the highest compliment that

I 3 could

could be paid a gentleman who was greatly favoured by the God of the Gardens — This pleafed his fancy fo much, that his choler inftantly fubfided, and he made no other reply, than—*Si c'étoit comme cela—à la bonheur.*

THE Cheval er being thus reconciled to Mis W——'s *jeu de mot,* foon after introduced M. Piz —— NI, the Venetian Refident. who took a fancy to this Lady; and now Mifs M—N had her revenge of Mrs. W——N, and called her lover W—N's *Pizzle* Nor was Mifs T—H without a limb of the Diplomatic Body, and though his name would not admit of a pun in the ludicrous ftile, it would admit of a very good fubftantial play, with the affiftance of an *r,* for indeed M. D'AG—o, the Genoefe Minifter, might with more propriety than either of the others, on account of his uncommon

mon generofity, be ftiled Monfieur *Ar-geno*, or rather *Argentum.*

WE might introduce the whole *Corps Diplomatique* of the Southern Depart-ment, fave the Spanifh Ambaffador, at FANNY's, but having given audience to thefe three gentlemen, we fhall for the prefent take our leave of abfence of them, and introduce Lord CHAMPETRE.

WE imagine there will be little occa-fion to pourtray the character of Lord CHAMPETRE, or to affign a reafon for his being thus entitled. Upon his mar-riage a fhort time fince with a Lady of uncommon beauty, whom he almoft idolized, he was prevailed upon by her to give a new fpecies of entertainment at the celebration of their nuptials. It confifted of a rural *Feftino*, where Art combined with Nature to make it one

of

of the moſt agreeable entertainments ever exhibited in this Country. The firſt nobility, and almoſt every perſon of any rank was invited to partake of the diverſion, and it ſurpaſſed even their moſt ſanguine expectations. The late Mr. GARRICK was ſo forcibly ſtruck with the enchanting ſcene, that he borrowed the hint for the Stage.

LADY CHAMPETRE for ſome time imitated all her amiable mother's virtues; but we are ſorry to add, that ſhe has ſince very materially deviated from ſo very worthy an example. The Noble Cricketer, it ſeems, was ſome time ſince ſuſpected of too cloſe an intimacy with this Lady; and her brother returned from his travels unexpectedly to enquire into the foundation of reports ſo diſhonourable to his ſiſter and to her family. But the Noble Cricketer poſitively

denying

denying he had in the least sullied the reputation of the Lady, or given any just cause for the injurious reports spread to her disadvantage, the D. of H. appeared satisfied. He however resolved carefully to watch his sister's motions; and her indiscretion soon became so glaring, that the polite circles of *St James*'s pronounced the Noble Cricketer the happy man; and at the same time talked as freely of Lord C—E, Mr. T—D, and Captain S—N.

A JAUNT she made last summer to *Brighthelmstone*, developed whatever remained of a mystery in her intrigues, and Lord CHAMPÊTRE at length had his eyes opened; and having had ocular demonstration of her infidelities, he is said to have written her the following billet:

I 5   " MADAM,

" Madam,

" UPON the receipt of this, you
" are defired to quit my houfe, and
" take what belongs to you, as your
" infamous *conduct*, of which I have
" had unqueftionable conviction, is too
" glaring and notorious for me to con-
" nive at."

This Card fhe found upon her toilet,
on her return from a caroufal with one
of her Enamoratos She judged it would
be in vain to remonftrate with her *cornuted caro fpofo*, but thought fhe could
fecure a friend with her mother, who
was tenderly fond of her but in this
opinion fhe was miftaken, as fhe had
been previoufly made acquainted with
her Daughter's infidelities, and had too
much reafon to believe they were
founded in truth In a word, the reception fhe met with at the D——fs of
A——le's. notwithftanding fhe had prepared

paied a fpecious apology for her conduct, pointed out to her there was no
other refource left foi her but to hide
her fhame in fome foreign country. She
accordingly foon after fet out for France
or Flandeis, wheie we believe fhe
now refides. We cannot pretend to
determine what will prove the fequel of this affair. Some affert that
the Noble Cricketer is fo enamoured
with Lady CHAMPETRE, that he has
promifed to give her his hand in an honourable way, as foon as fhe is legally
difunited fiom her prefent hufband.
We muft, however, leave this matter
at picfent in fufpence, and wait upon
his Lordfhip at Mis. BRADSHAW's,
where we have rather unpolitely left him
fo long, after having regulaily introduced him.

*CHAP. XXXVI.

Strong Suspicions of a Connexion between Lord CHAMPETRE and Mrs. BR-DSH-W. His first Meeting with Mrs. ARMST—D His Proposals to her, which are accepted. His Lordsh-p is supposed still to have a Penchant for FANNY Some Account of Mrs BR—DSH—W's other Visitors, with some Description of their Persons. A whimsical, but genuine Anecdote, &c. &c. &c.

IT was at Mrs. BR—DSH—W's that Lord CHAMPETRE first saw Mrs. ARMST—D. It is the general opinion that Lord CHAMPETRE had a *tendre* for FANNY, and that he occasionally consecrated at the shrine of Venus in her arms. Thus much is certain, he used frequently to visit at Mrs. BR—D-SH—W's.

sH—w's, when there was no other often-
fible object of attraction; and that she
has been feen in his carriage in the environs of the town, and upon the different roads leading to *Richmond, Putney,*
and *Hampftead.* But Mrs ARMST—D
being a Vifitor at Mrs. BRADSHAW's, he
directed his falacious artillery, and planted it point blank, at this Lady, who foon
yielded, upon a *carte blanche* being offered her by way of capitulation. She
had all the honours of amorous war allowed her, and yielded *tambour battant,*
meche allumée. We beg, however, that
the Reader may not put a falfe con-
ftruction upon this laft expreffion, and
think that there was the leaft reafon to
fufpect a *firebrand* on either fide.

MANY are of opinion, that his Lordfhip ftill continues to entertain a *penchant*
for

for FANNY, though she is now at least fifty, and that he divides his affections between her and Mrs. ARMST——D. Be this as it may, the Ladies associate with the most perfect cordiality, and there does not appear to be one scruple of jealousy between them.

As we have given an outline of FANNY's pursuits prior to her present situation, it will probably be expected that we should pay the same attention to Mrs. ARMST——D.

WE are informed that Mrs. ARMST——D claims no higher ancestry than being the descendant of a Cordwainer, who commenced an itinerant Methodist-preacher; that being deserted by her parents, and having no kind of support, she judged it prudent to set her charms up to sale; and that excellent Negociatress
Mrs.

Mrs. GOADBY having undertaken to vend them at a good market, she gave a bill of sale of them to a Jew Merchant. At this period, it seems, she was not above nineteen, elegant in her person, and beautiful in the *contour* of her physiognomy, and the symmetry of her features. It is averred that Lord L——N was the next admirer to whom she was introduced afterwards, but that his Lordship's finances not being at that time in so flourishing a state as he could have wished, she found but little pecuniary advantages from his acquaintance, and judged it prudent to bestow her company upon the Duke of A———. This correspondence continued some months, till he discovered her infidelity to him; and a short time after we find her in the embraces of the Noble Cricketer. Singular as this may appear, considering his future connexion with Lady CHAMPETRE, it

has

has been pretty well authenticated ; and it may be faid upon this occafion, that the Duke and his Lordfhip only charged partners in the fame Cotillon.

Soon after Lord CHAMPETRE framed this correfpondence with Mrs. ARMST—D, he took a neat villa for her near *Hamp-ftcad*, and this Lady and FANNY paffed the greater part of laft fummer at this rural retreat, making occafional excur-fions in his Lordfhip's carriage to the Watering-places and Races.

THIS connexion is now fo well ef-tablifhed, and his Lordfhip preferving not the leaft fecrecy upon the occafion, there is reafon to believe it will be of long duration, and that he by turns finds all his amorous paffions giatified in the arms of FANNY HE—BE—T and Mrs. ARMST—D. Befides the vifits of Lord

Lord CHAMPETRE, FANNY was frequently favoured with the company of Colonel B—, Sir Thomas L—, Lord B—, and many of the Members of ARTHUR's and BOOTLE's. The Ladies who ufually frequented her were CHARLOTTE SP—R, who derived this name from her connexion with Lord SP—R H—N, Mifs G—LLE, Mifs MAS—N, Mrs. T—R, and Mrs. L—NE.

THE firft of thefe Ladies has for fome years been upon the lift of fiift-rate Courtezans, though fhe is ftill in her piime, and is a very elegant figure. She is very choice in her admiffion of lovers; and though fhe has had a great variety, fhe always prefers her old acquaintance to new faces. Lord B—— is very fond of CHARLOTTE, though he has known her upwards of fix years. His Lordfhip is not now the gay *beaulgar* çon of two-and-twenty, as was NED H——, when he made a conqueſt of a certain Ducheſs at *Tunbridge*; and he finds there is more trouble in coming at *Tidbits*, than in coming to action with a Lady of experience, who is free of acceſs and open to every onſet, though perhaps not ſo vigorous as a juvenile attack.

As Lord B——'s adventure at *Tunbridge* was both lucky and whimſical, we think the Reader will not be diſpleaſed to meet with it here. At that time the Rooms were kept by Mr. TOY, who, on account of an heſitation in his voice, and beginning all his ſentences with *Tit Tit*, let the firſt word be whatever it might, was nick-named *Tit Tit*. The Ducheſs of M—— was that ſeaſon at the Wells, when walking in

the

the Gardens, she espied through a bush a most extraordinary Sensitive Plant, which her Grace soon discovered to be *Tit Tit*'s. It so struck her with the length and size, that she resolved to be mistress of it, and even went so far as to offer Toy her hand, but unfortunately he was engaged, and could not accept of the honour proposed to be conferred upon him. However, surmising the cause of her Grace's fondness, he having perceived her at the instant that she had viewed the Sensitive Plant, and willing to do his friend NED a service, he informed her Grace, that this Gentleman was in possession of a still finer Plant than himself, and still more sensitive. This intimation tickled her Grace's——*fancy*, and in a short time we find Ned in the full possession of her——*fortune*.

MISS

Miss G——LLE, the next upon the catalogue of female visitors, is a tall genteel girl, about nineteen: she has a remarkably sweet expressive countenance, which is a just index of her natural good temper. She is the daughter of a Clergyman, who dying when she was young, left no provision for her support, except the subscription for the benefit of the Sons and Daughters of the Clergy; and she was from this Fund placed an apprentice to a mantua-maker. She served part of her time; but an Attorney's Clerk paying his addresses to her, as she imagined upon honourable terms, she was induced to take a trip to *Scotland* with him; but upon the road he having the rhetoric to persuade her to antedate the ceremony, after two nights gratification he took a French leave, and she was obliged to get back

... this the coud-grcatly ...rified
at the difappointment, ...
pointed out the road to gain a ......
hood; and having given up her p.e-
tenfions to chaftity, and being introduced to Mrs. NELSON, fhe was eafily
perfuaded to follow her dictates, and
commence a boarder at her-houfe.

MISS MAS—N is defcended from a
Family who lived far beyond their income, imagining there was no occafion
to make any provifion for her,
as fhe had in the eyes of her parents
fufficient charms to entitle her to a hufband of rank and fortune; but alas!
the men of this period think beauty is
always to be purchafed when attended
with poverty, and this Lady was a cor-
roboratirg inftance of the truth of this
obfervation.

Mrs.

Mrs. Tur—r is daughter of a capital linen-draper, who upon his demife left her a very genteel fortune, upon which fhe for fome time lived in affluence; but unfortunately meeting with Mr. Tur—r (who was a profeffed fortune-hunter, and had already deceived many credulous women in the fame fituation as he did this lady), and he offering his hand in marriage, after a fhort courtfhip fhe yielded to his folicitations. But fcarce had the honey-moon elapfed, ere he de-camped, having gained poffeffion of her bonds and effects, and fhe learnt too late that he had, previous to her marriage, at leaft half-a-dozen wives then living. In phrenzy and defpair, fhe now refolved to make reprifals upon the whole Male Sex, and raife contributions upon every one fhe met with. Nor has fhe been unfuccefsful in this refpect, having

having in the courſe of about eighteen months, by labouring in her preſent vocation, realized near 1500*l.*

Mrs. L—NE is a very pretty little woman, with black eyes and jetty locks. She is about five-and-twenty, and has for ſome time reſided in *New-Compton-Street*, at N⁰ 10. We acknowledge, we are not much acquainted with her hiſtory, but believe ſhe ſerved her time to a Millener near *Leiceſter-Fields*. She is far from being mercenary, and is a chatty, agreeable female.

Such are the principal viſitants of Mrs. BRADSHAW, of whom we ſhall now take leave, after ſo long a viſit.

CHAP.

*C H A P. XXXVII.

A Visit to Mrs PENDERGAST's. *An Account of a capricious Amour, in which Lord* FUMBLE *was the capital Actor. Unexpected Consequences, very alarming to his Lordship. The judicious Steps taken to prevent farther disagreeable Effects. Their Success. A feu de joye, Rejoicings and Illuminations, upon a very extraordinary Occasion.*

MRS. PENDERGAST's house is in the center of *King's-Place*, and has hitherto kept up its dignity under the regulations of this judicious Lady Abbess. Some of the finest Nymphs under the denomination of *filles de joye* have figured in this Seminary, and entertained some of the first Nobility; but an unlucky affair that happened a few months

4   since

since in this Nunnery, had nearly destroyed all its reputation. The story is as follows: Old Lord FUMBLE, of the Stable-Yard, used constantly to visit this house three times a-week, since the demise of the late Mrs. JOHNSON of St. James's-Place, who knew to a tittle how to tickle his Lordship's fancy, but her loss was almost irreparable, and it was for some time before Lord FUMBLE could find an Abbess, who could hit his fancies and caprices like Mother JOHNSON However, Mrs. PENDERGAST being recommended to his Lordship by Sii ROGER ALLPOP, he accompanied the Baronet one evening to this receptacle of prostituted beauty; but notwithstanding Mrs. PENDERGAST herself was willing to leave no stone unturned to please his Lordship; the elegant Mrs. D—E—LD was introduced; the pretty NANCY AMB—SE succeeded her, and was followed by the sparkling Amelia Coz--ns, His Lordship said, they were not his taste. A messenger was accordingly instantly dispatched to Mrs. Butler, in the Sanctuary, *Westminster*, who usually had some Country young Tits in training for Mrs. Pendergast's immediate service. In a short time two of them arrived, decked out by Mrs. Butler. Lord Fumble greatly approved of them, and having ordered them to undress, began his manual operations, which were succeeded by theirs. In fine, at the length of about an hour, his Lordship *fancied* he had been highly gratified, and recompensed them for their trouble with three guineas each. These Ladies went by the names of Country Bet and Black Susan, but had, as it afterwards appeared, a diversity of names. They expected a much larger prefent, confidering the accounts they had received of Lord FUMBLE's generofity; and they thought they had earned their prefent with great labour and much difficulty, to bring his Lordfhip to the zeft of his amorous paffion.

Upon their return to the Sanctuary, Mother BUTLER demanded what fhe called Poundage; in other words, five fhillings in every pound Foolifh Black SUSAN readily complied; but Country BET knew the value of fifteen fhillings too well, and peremptorily refufed. But unfortunately having, during the conteft, ftripped herfelf of her finery, and prepared to reaffume her ufual garb, Mother BUTLER laid an embargo on her clothes. This fo enraged Country BET, that fhe repaired the fame night to the Rotation-Office in *Litchfeld-fireet*, and obtained a warrant for

K 2   Mrs.

Mrs Butler. This curious examination has been given in the public papers by a person who was present, and we cannot better illustrate the adventure, than by quoting *verbatim* his relation.

" Monday the 10th of November
" 1778, at the Rotation-Office *Litchfield-*
" *Street*, Elizabeth Clumpet, *alias*
" Cummings, otherwise Country Bet,
" appeared before the Magistrates, and
" charged a Mrs. Butler, who keeps a
" house of ill fame in the Sanctuary,
" *Westminster*, with keeping a gown,
" handkerchief, &c. which she had left
" at her house, instead of a dress But-
" ler had furnished her with, to go in
" company with another woman of the
" lowest order, to meet the Earl of
" H——, at the house of Mrs. Pender-
" gast, who keeps a Seraglio in *King's-*
" *Place*; which clothes Butler would

" not

" not deliver until the girl had paid her
" the ufual Poundage out of her wages
" of iniquity. SPENCER SMITH, a Ser-
" jeant in the firſt regiment of grena-
" diers, appeared in behalf of Mrs. But-
" LER; ſaid ſhe was his wife, and that
" he was her ſecond huſband, but ſhe
" went by the name of BUTLER, and
" endeavoured to overthrow the evi-
" dence againſt her. However, Cou
" BET being, interrogated
" Bench, declared the Serjeant's wife
" frequently furniſhed the Seraglio
" King's-Place with Ladies which ſhe
" picked up, dreſſed as maids, and ſent
" them as above; that the Earl of H——
" attended there on Sundays, Mondays,
" Wedneſdays, and Fridays, each of
" which days he was there laſt week;
" and that this Procureſs inſtructed her
" and her companion (his Lordſhip hav-
" ing two females with him at a time)
" how to behave, and dreſſed them up

K 3   " like

" like *maids of fashion*. She likewife
" added, the noble Earl (in whofe com-
" pany they were half an hour) gave
" them fix guineas; that SMITH was as
" bad as his wife in this iniquitous bu-
" finefs, and that he himfelf, after they
" were properly equipped, fetched a
" coach for them to wait on his Lord-
" fhip It being proved to the fatif-
" faction of the Magiftrates, that BUT-
" LER, *alias* SMITH, keeps an infamous
" houfe, Country BET was bound over
" to profecute at the next *Weftminfter*
" Seffions."

No fooner had this adventure appeared in the public News-Papers, than
Lord H——, *alias* FUMBLE, flew upon
the wings of paffion, (that is to fay,
as faft as he could hobble along) to
Mrs. PENDERGAST. His Lordfhip ftut-
tered, fwore, ftammered and ftamped
with his cane, till he was quite out of
breath,

breath, before he could get a word from the immaculate hostess. At length, being quite out of breath, he threw himself upon a sopha, and then was compelled to listen to Mrs. PENDER-GAST's defence.

"INDEED, my good, my noble Lord, "you surprise me beyond any thing I "have ever heard in my life. The little "Brimstone!, to refuse paying Pound-"age, and then go to the Rotation-Office, "and expose my house, and, what is "more, your Lordship's whims and ca-"prices, which every Nobleman has a "right to indulge himself in, especially "when he pays for them, aye, and "handsomely too. She shall never en-"ter my door again, as long as she "breathes, I'll teach her to reveal se-"crets, and that upon oath too, before "a parcel of foolish *Justices*, who think,

"like

" like Mechanics, that no man—no,—
" not even a Peer of the Realm has a
" right to enjoy any other woman than
" his wife, and that in the old John
" Trot-way, as Adam and Eve did in
" Paradife. But——"

" But," refumed Lord Fumble, "hold
" your damned clatter! What is to be
" done? If we do not ftop this Wench's
" mouth, I fhall be hauled over the coals
" again in a Court of Juftice, and become
" the butt and ridicule of all the World!
" —Why, I fhall not be able to fhew my
" face at Court, or even to my own fer-
" vants."

" Leave it to me, my Lord! I'll go
" this inftant, find out the foolifh, impu-
" dent B—h, and ftop her mouth fo ef-
" fectually, that fhe will not proceed
" any farther in this bufinefs."

" Aye,

" Aye, but there is another ftep ne-
" ceffary to be taken, to prevent this
" d—n'd affair being propagated as
" little as poffible."

" What is that, my Lord?"

" Why, you muft fend Emiffaries to
" all parts of the Town, to buy up every
" Paper that can be got at, which con-
" tains any account of this *Litchfield-*
" *Street* bufinefs ; and others muft be
" difpatched to all the Coffee-houfes,
" where they take in thefe papers, and
" they muft pocket them and bring them
" off, let the rifk be what it will."

" Your Lordfhip's commands," faid
Mrs. Pendergast, " fhall be punctual-
" ly and inftantly obeyed," and in lefs
than half-an-hour, fhe had difpatched
half-a-dozen meffengers upon this bufi-

nefs.

nefs. In a few hours they returned with many quires of purchafed and ftolen News-Papers. Mrs. PENDERGAST, on her part, fet off immediately for the Sanctuary, and in a fhort time difcovered Country BET's retreat. She accordingly repaired thither, and after a fhort conference, BET agreed to drop the profecution for five guineas. After fhe had put her mark to this agreement, Mrs. PENDERGAST returned home, and difpatched a meffenger to acquaint his Lordfhip with the glad tidings. He was then in a melancholy mood, ruminating in his clofet upon the ridiculous figure he had that day made ; and which had induced him to keep from Court, as well as the Chocolate-houfe. But no fooner did he receive this difpatch, than he ordered his chair to *King's-Place,* to have a conference with Mrs. PENDER-

GAST

GAST upon the occasion He was greatly pleased to see Mrs Burler indemni-
fied from the profecution, and was ftill
more rejoiced to fee fo large a bundle of
News Papers, (collected partly by ftra-
tagem) in which his folly, if not his in-
famy was inrolled; and in the fullnefs of
his heart, ordered a bonfire immediately
to be made of them in the Court, and a
butt of porter to be given to the populace.
Many people thought that fome important good news had arrived, that we had
either completely defeated Washing-
ton or taken D'Orvilliers' whole fleet
Had it been the night of terminating
Admiral Keppel's Trial, it would probably have had as rapid an effect, as Par-
ker the Printer illuminating his houfe
upon the arrival of the meffenger with
the account of the Admiral's honourable
acquittal. As it was, it turned out to

K 6   fome

fome advantage to the Tallow chan-
dlers, as many houfes were illuminated
in confequence of this fignal, particularly all the Nunneries in *King's-Place*

CHAP.

*C H A P. XXXVIII.

The Meſures taken by Mrs. PENDER-
GAST *for recovering the Reputation of
her Seminary. Her uncommon Svcceſs; a
Subſcription being ſet on foot for a new
Species of Entertainment, in which are
blended the Sports of* Venus, *and the Rites
of* Bacchus, *and Lord* FUMBLE *ſub-
ſcribes nobly in conſequence of his late
Good-luck. Some Account of the* Bal
d'Amour. *A Deſcription of the Ladies, and their Charaĉters A whimſical Rencontre between Lords* G— *and*
L—, *and Ladies* G— *and* L——. *A
mortifying Situation to Lord* PYEBALD,
&c. &c. &c.*

NOTWITHSTANDING the *fea
de joye* and illuminations we mentioned in the laſt Chapter, Mrs. PEN-

DEPGAST was very far from being re-conciled to the misfortune that had given rise to it. She plainly foresaw, that it would be very prejudicial to her house, as Noblemen and Gentlemen would be fearful of coming thither, lest they should be exposed in a similar manner to Lord FUMB E. She judged it adviseable to write a circular letter to all her customers, to assure them, that such an accident should for the future be carefully prevented; that the girl who had given rise to this casualty was banished for ever from her house; and that Mrs BUTLER, on account of her imprudence, in letting matters get to such a crisis, should never be employed again as Deputy Procuress to her Seminary she at the same time intimated, that on the Wednesday evening following, there would be a diversion quite out of the common *routine*, under the title of *Bal d'Amour*,

* *d'Amour*, where some of the finest Women in Europe would make their appearance, masked indeed, but in other respects *in puris naturalibus*. The hint was, doubtless, taken from CHARLOTTE HAYES's Rites of Venus, as performed at Otaheite; but Mrs. PENDERGAST'S inventive genius soon pointed out to her many improvements that had a very happy effect.

HAVING taken this previous step, she now dispatched messengers to every fine

---

* Many of our Readers have imagined that the hint of the *Bal d'Amour* was taken from a famous *Coterie* in former ages, instituted at Rome, and consecrated to the *Bona Dea*; but it should be remembered, that all Male-Visitors were there publicly excluded. It is true, that *Claudius* and some few other peculiar favourites were admitted; but a general invitation, similar to this, never took place.

woman

woman or pretty girl that fhe could depend upon, and who would liften to the
fummons, within the Bills of Mortality;
and many of them accepted the invitation. Among thefe were Lady AD—MS,
from *Litchfield Street*, a fine black wo-
man· Mifs ST-TON, from *Red-lion-Street*,
Holborn, who was genteel, handfome,
and engaging: Mifs M-LLS, from *New-
Street*, a fine girl with a very harmonious voice· M·fs G—LDSMITH, from
Caftle-Court ; elegant in perfon, and
extremely good-natured· Mifs M—T-
CHELL, from *Crown Court, Bow-Street*,
fhe is fhort but genteel, with a happy arrangement of regular features
Mifs L—MBERT, from *St. Martin's-
Street*; a middle-fized fair girl, with enchanting blue eyes, and uncommonly
elegant in her drefs and appearance·
Mifs OLIV—R, from *Frith-Street, Soho*;

3   fhe

she unites innocence, sweetness and simplicity: Miss L——DG—R, from *May-Fair*; uncommonly sumptuous in her dress, and magnificent in her manner: Miss W—K—NSON, from *Prince's-Court George-Street*, in keeping by the Swedish Amb—r; she is plain, but has a certain *je ne scai quoi* that is altogether irresistible.

HAVING secured these Ladies upon their parole of Honour, she now waited in person upon all her friends and customers, either at their own houses, or, if they were in a connubial state, at the Chocolate-house; and every one who agreed to attend the *Bal d'Amour* subscribed at least five guineas Some gave her a Bank-note, others a Rouleau, and Lord FUMBLE in particular, gave her fifty guineas. By these means she had now in her possession above seven hundred
dred

dred guineas, whereby she was enabled to make preparations suitable to the occasion. She provided a good band of music, who were so disposed, as to afford their harmonious assistance, without being admitted spectators of the festive scene An elegant cold collation was also prepared, with wines of all kinds in abundance.

THE evening of this *Gala*, *Pall Mall* was thronged with chairs and carriages, and every one seemed emulous who should first enter the Paphian Temple. Besides the THAIS's we have already mentioned and described, Lady G——R and Lady L——R came in disguise; and, in justice to these Ladies, it must be acknowledged, that they preserved more decency than the rest of the female Votaries of VENUS; as they appeared like our Great Grand-Mother EVE, and covered their countenances with large

fig.

fig-leaves. No fooner had they made
their appearance thus habited, than
there was fuch a hue and cry for fig-
leaves, that it was neceffary to fend for
a cargo from *Covent Garden* Market.
The BIRD of PARADISE was alfo prefent,
with a curious *Cyprian Fly-Cap*, as fhe
called it, fo furbelowed and tambour-
ed, as to afford a very pleafing effect,
the figures and devices being truly em-
blematical of, the occafion, and fhe
could perform every natural office, without difcompofing it—this fly-cap being
judicioufly perforated in the centre:
and it was particularly ufeful in preventing chafing, either by friction, or the
lofs of a fingle hair in dancing, a circumftance that difpleafed Baron N——N,
as it was his peculiar and whimfical con-
cupifcence to roll a candle up and down
the Saloon, during the paufe of every
dance, to determine to whom belonged
every

every particular hair that had fallen from the feat of blifs, by the motion and exercife of the dance.

AFTER they had danced about a couple of hours, the cold collation was announced, and each Gentleman conducted his partner to the feftive board; where having amply regaled themfelves, and drunk about half a dozen toafts to the honour of the Cyprian Goddefs and all her Rites—the fcene changed, and prefented a *camera objcura*, with a proper number of fophas, to realize thofe Rites which had been celebrated only in theory.

THE fervency of the devotion, upon this occafion, could fcarcely be paralleled, and it is fomewhat extraordinary, that Lord G——R and Lord L——R enjoyed their own wives without knowing

ing it; and, ftrange to tell! pronounced their imaginary LAIS's moft excellent Pieces. It was thought, upon the difcovery, which was made the enfuing morning, that this would have been the means of promoting a reconciliation between the parties. Indeed, a rumour was circulated throughout the Town, that all mifunderftanding had ceafed between Lord G——R and his Lady; and that they actually cohabited again together. As to Lord L——R and his Lady, this expectation was rendered abortive, by his Lady having (*innocently*, we will fuppofe) in this amorous conflict, once more conferred upon his Lordfhip a certain *Neapolitan* complaint; a favour which fhe had received a few days before from a Foreign Minifter, much efteemed amongft the Ladies for his uncommon parts and amorous abilities.

Upon the whole, this unparalleled entertainment gave such general satisfaction, that at the request of all present it was to be repeated that day fortnight; and it was expected it would be far more numerous than upon the first occasion. Every Lady of *easy virtue* was complimented with three guineas, besides her chair-hire. Some of the Ladies refused any pecuniary gratification; and by that means distinguished themselves from the Grizettes, who were compelled to yield to necessity. Lady G———r, Lady L.———r, and the Bird of Paradise, in particular, rejected receiving the money offered them, but politely delired Mrs. Pendergast to give it to the servants. Lady Ad———ms said she should pocket the affront, which created a general laugh, as it was imagined she would upon this occasion make use of a

certain

certain *Niche*, which had been fufficiently dilated by the Duke of Q———y
to have held a hundred guineas inftead
of three, but the company were difap-
pointed in this refpect, for fhe only
flipt the money into her glove. The
Duke of A——r very geneioufly prefented Mifs Ol——ver with a twenty
pound Bank note, faying, he believed
that the Marchionefs of C———n had
either ftudied under Mifs Ol—ver, or
this Lady under the Marchionefs, for
that their movements were fo very fimi-
lar, and their pantings and heavings
fo much alike, that he fancied himfelf
all the while in the arms of his dear
Marchionefs, in fearch of whom he
came thither; but that Mifs Ol——ver
had fo well fupplied her place, as to
render the difappointment quite fup-
portable.

COUNT

COUNT H—o made a very respectable figure, but did not come to action; saying to Miss ST—TON, in French, "*Que de baiser trop fut très perni-* "*cieux à la santé.*" It was not a little mortifying for Lord PYEBALD to be seated next to the Count, as the contrast of their *parts* was very striking;—and Lady L—R asked his Lordship, "If " he was always so well equipped for " amorous sports?" This cutting question made the *Sensitive Plant* shrink almost to nothing, and his Lordship was obliged to retire, the laugh was so intolerable against him.

THIS well-concerted plan of Mrs. PENDERGAST not only restored the dignity of her house, but by this *Bal d'Amour*, and the repetition of it, she put near a thousand pounds in her pocket, and was pronounced to be the

proper

proper fucceffor of Mrs. Corn—lys, as the Emprefs of Tafte and Luxury.

We fhall now leave Mrs. Pender-gast to enjoy the fruits of her genius, and the renovation of her cuftom, in defpite of Mrs. Butler and Country Bet, the *Litchfield-Street* Magiftrates, or Lord Fumble's difgrace; and pay our next vifit to Mrs. Windsor, in due fuc-ceffion of order and etiquette.

*C H A P. XXXIX.

A Visit to Mrs. WINDSOR. Some Account of the Reputation of the House. An Error that has prevailed, with regard to the Identity of Mrs. WINDSOR's Person, and its pernicious Effects. Description of the Nuns of this Seminary, in the Persons of Miss BETSY K—NG, Miss NEWSH—M, Miss MERED—TH, and Mrs. WILL—MS; with some curious Anecdotes of this Lady, and a certain amorous Squire, of Hackney. The Artifices of his Pimp delineated. The Cause of her Marriage, and its Consequences.

A SIMILITUDE of name between this Lady and another Female who lives not a hundred miles from

Wardour-

Wardour-Street, Soho, has induced many of her well-meaning friends to shun the house, as reports have been pretty currently spread, that the latter of these women is addicted to such practices as shock human nature, and which make us shudder at the very suggestion; and we would recommend to this Lady to change her name, at least the brazen inscription upon her door, that all imputations of this enormous kind may be taken off from her friends and visitors.

We find at Mrs. WINDSOR's some very good Pieces, who have many admirers. Amongst these are BETSY K—G, a fine sparkling girl about nineteen, who may be said to be as attractive a Thais as any within the purlieus of *King's-Place.* Her person can only be paralleled by her behaviour, which is completely amiable; and if you can for

a moment

a moment forget that fhe is compelled to proftitute her fweet perfon for hire, you might almoft imagine her an Angel. She was feduced, when at a Boarding-fchool, by Black HARRIET, who was then in her profperity; but it muft be acknowledged, that fhe did not ufe fuch artifices as SANTA CHARLOTTA did with refpect to Mifs M——E, from B—— L——, or Mrs. N—LS—N with regard to Mifs W—MS and Mifs J—NES. It is true, that fhe was the negociator of the treaty between her and Lord B——E; but BETSY met her almoft half-way, and declared fhe was tired to remain in pof-feffion of half a Maidenhead;—for that by the practices of her fchool-fellows, fhe had acquired fuch knowledge in the art of Mafturbation, as to gratify her paffions almoft to excefs; but that, in-ftead of making her neglect the thoughts of real blifs, it only induced her to

pant

pant the more eagerly for the real enjoyment of a fine fellow, and Lord B—e being reprefented to her in this light, and as armed at all points to make a woman completely happy, fhe readily yielded to his embrace, upon the firft interview Her elopement from fchool created an alarm, and when her uncle, who was her neareft relation living, found fhe was debauched, and a refident of *King's-Place*, he, to fpeak in the vulgar phrafe, wafhed his hands of her. Thus fituated, Lord B—e's paffion having foon fubfided, fhe found herfelf under the neceffity of proftituting her charms, and admitting a variety of Lovers.

MISS N—w—m is another favourite Lais in Mrs. WINDSOR's Seminary. This young Lady is tall and genteel, with fine expreffive eyes, and moft

beautiful

beautiful treffes, that require no art to set them off to advantage. A merchant in *Lothbury* frequently vifits her, and allows her a very handfome income, by which fhe might fupport herfelf in a very genteel manner, but the ambition of fplendour, and an infatiable luft for drefs and fafhionable amufements, hurry her into company that fhe defpifes, and fometimes loathes,—but as money is an all-powerful argument with NEW—M, fhe cannot refift the powers of its temptation, whenever it comes in her way. Whether it is SOUBISE, or Little ISAAC from *St. Mary Axe*, the fpankers will prevail; and fhe fays, fhe cannot difcover more fin in yielding to a Blackamoor or a Jew, than to a Chriftian, or even a Methodift.

MRS. WINDSOR lately fuftained a very confiderable lofs, in the perfon of Mifs MERE—TH,

MERE—TH, a Welch young Lady, who attracted Sir W—TK—NS W—; W—, Lord B———Y, and moſt of the Welch Noblemen and Gentlemen, when in Town, ſhe being conſtructed entirely to the taſte of Ancient Britons; and it is pretty generally known, that the females of that country are modelled differently from the Engliſh Ladies, and that the Seat of Bliſs is placed ſome inches higher in front, and far more diſtant from a neighbouring conveyance, than our women. A certain Baronet, who lives in the North of England, having fixed his eye upon Miſs MER—DITH, immediately conceived an idea, that ſhe was framed exactly to his purpoſe. The Baronet's eſtate was a little out at the elbows, and in order to repair it, he was in purſuit of a place. A certain Great Man in power was to pay him a viſit in a few days, in the country.

L 4 He

He knew the Minister's weak side—he could not refift the temptation of Women—he had defcribed a Welch girl who had afforded him the greateft raptures of any of her fex; and, according to his defcription, fhe very clofely refembled Mifs MERE—TH. The Baronet accordingly entered into a treaty with this Lady, and fpeedily came to a conclufion. He agreed to take her into keeping, conftitute her his houfe keeper, and in cafe he fhould die before her, leave her a handfome annuity. The bait was tempting, and fhe could not refift its influence. A life of variegated proftitution had given her a furfeit of Modern Nunneries, and the propofal made her was entirely agreeable to her mind. Accordingly fhe fet off with the Baronet in his poft-chaife for *Yorkfhire*, and arrived at his Manfion two days after. Every thing correfponded with

his

his defcription, and all the *agrémens* weie perfectly confonant to his promifes.

THREE days after the Great Man arriv-ed, and he was quite fmitten with the charms of Mifs MERE—TH. The Baronet now threw off the mafk, and told her he had made her fortune. The Minifter im-med ately gave her a finecure, as Houfe-keeper to one of the Public-Offices, which brought in near three hundred a-year. She was aftonifhed at the Bá-ronet's turning pimp upon the occafion : but looking over the Papers, in a few days after, found his name tacked to a poft of confiderable value and import-ance. The myftery was revealed, and fhe was very well fatisfied with this un-expected change, which was far more advantageous than any thing fhe could expect from the Baronet ; as his affairs, fhe difcovered, were in a critical fitua-

tion,

t'on, and that this *manœuvre* became neceſſary to replace him upon his legs.

Mrs. C. W——ms, however, ſtill remained with Mrs. Windsor; and ſhe was an object deſerving of attention. She had not been long in Town, and might be conſidered as a new Piece. She had been a ſervant-maid to the celebrat-ed Mr. T——, of *Hackney*, ſo famous for his variegated amours, and uncom-mon feats of gallantry, by the aſſiſtance of his unwieldy Pandar, who is ſaid to poſſeſs the art of perſuaſion, and cor-rupting female innocence, beyond any Lady Abbeſs in *England*. He met Miſs W——ms one day in *Smithfield*, and perceiving her to be a fine, freſh, bloom-ing country girl, thought ſhe would ſuit his maſter to a nicety. He accord-ingly accoſted her; and finding ſhe was come to *London* in ſearch of a place, told

hei

her he could recommend her to one of
the best places in all the world; and if
she would step into the next inn, he
would give her the direction. The innocent girl seeing a well-looking elderly
man, in a laced waistcoat, a fine flaxen
perriwig, and every thing about him
corresponding with her notion of a gentleman, did not hesitate going and par-
taking of a pint of wine. Ere the de-
canter was emptied, he found out that
she was that very day come to Town,
and was not yet provided with a lodging.
This discovery was highly opportune,
and he told her that as this was the case,
the best thing she could do, was to get
her box from the adjacent inn, and that
he would take her down to *Hackney* in
his chaise, which was then ready in the
Yard, and in which he was going to return in a few minutes. The girl was
greatly rejoiced in being so speedily and
so

fo well provided for, as the profpect feemed to teftify; and accordingly accepted of F——'s offer—got into the chaife with him, and was whirled down to *Hackney* in a trice.

Upon his arrival at the Squire's houfe, he was abfent; but knowing the Inn he frequented, F— immediately fent for him; and in the interim ordered out the cold victuals, by way of refrefhment, as well for himfelf as his fellow-traveller. Upon T—'s arrival, he was highly delighted with his new gueft, hired her immediately, and gave her more wages than fhe afked.

His trufty Duenna foon perfuaded her to yield to his amorous embraces, faying he would certainly marry her; and ufed fo many perfuafions, and well-timed prefents, as quite intoxicated the innocent

cent girl, who really fancied she should soon be Mrs. T——— in reality. Some months elapsed after this, and she proved pregnant. T—n now being tired of her, hit upon a device to get rid of her, which was to marry her to his groom, and set them up in a little public-house in the *Borough*. Wil- l—ms, her husband, turned out an idle, drunken fellow, and in a short time found his way to the *King's-Bench* Prison. An execution coming into the house, compelled her to quit it, and once more seek her fortune at large One of Mrs. Windsor's Runners having given her intimation of Mrs. Wil- liams's situation, she soon introduced herself to her. The consequence was, upon an invitation to *King's-Place*, Mrs. W—ms was speedily initiated into all the Arcana of this Seminary, where she still continues, and is one of Mrs. Wind- sor's best assistants.

CHAP.

• C H A P. XL.

A descriptive Account of Mrs. R—DS—N's House of genteel Intrigue. Outline of the Characters of Mrs. R—DS—N's principal Visitors. An unexpected visit from a certain zalorous Duke. A very curious Scale of Female Continence and Incontinence, approved, as it is said, ere now, by a certain great and learned Society. The Arrival of Sir W. B. and Lord S; and the Danger of the luminous Appearance of a certain Nautical Commander.

WE think it incumbent on us to introduce our Reader at Mrs. R—DS—N's near *Bolton-Street, Piccadilly.* This Lady professes the *Bon Ton* in its greatest refinement; so we find she admits no female visitors who frequent

the

the Nunneries, or are to be obtained at a minute's warning by a meſſage from a gentleman-porter at the *Bedford Arms*, or a runner from *Maltby*'s. Her female friends conſiſt of either women in high keeping, or married Ladies, who come in diſguiſe to amuſe themſelves with a *Beau Garçon*, and water the horns, that they may continue growing and thriving, and which they had before planted up-on their dear, ſweet (IMPOTENT) huſ-bands brows. We accordingly, at one time, find her houſe frequented by Mrs. T——, whoſe intimate acquaintance with the late F—th—r of the C—ty, was pretty well known. This Lady, though rather paſt the prime of life, is ſtill actuated by amorous paſſions; and ſince the demiſe of her friend Sir R— L——, ſhe has yield-ed to the impulſe of her inclinations, and reſolves to make the moſt of the re-mainder of the ſpan of life in amorous dalliance.

dalliance. Lord P—y met her here once, when rather inebriate; and being informed that Mrs T—s was a very fine woman, and in her prime; thinking himself rather impofed upon in the latter part of the affertion, rudely faid to Mrs. T—s, " Pray, Madam, will you be fo " kind as to inform me, at what time of " life a woman's amorous paffions fub- " fide?" " Indeed, my Lord," fhe faid, " you fhould afk that queftion of a wo- " man far older than myfelf:—but this I " can fay, it frequently happens, that " a man's amorous abilities fail him " before he is out of his *teens*."

MRS. M—SH, a Lady whom Lord PYEBALD has maintained for many years, frequently vifits Mrs. R—DS—N's, to tafte of thofe joys which his Lordfhip has, for a confiderable time, forgot to put her in mind of; and fhe thinks a *rouleau*

though

though her whole monthly allowance,
not too much for an evening's gratification with Enfign PAT—N.

Mifs KEN—DY is, another Lady who
frequents this rendezvous. This Enamo-
ra'a is fo well known for her amours,
and the intereft fhe took in faving her
Brothers from an untimely end, that it
were needlefs to dwell upon her character. fuffice it, to fay, that fhe does not
come here to difpofe of her *rouleaus*, but
in order to gain fome, if poffible. But as
her charms are rather upon the wane fhe
thinks it prudent not to refufe five guineas when offered to her   This Lady has
been fo long accuftomed to a freedom of
fpeech bordering upon the indelicate,
that fhe fometimes offends the chafte
ears of even Mrs. R—DS—N. The
truth is, nothing tickles this Lady's fancy more than a good bouncing *double*, or
even

even *single entendre*. As a proof of this affertion, we shall give a short anecdote concerning her. Being some time since in the gallery at the *Old-Bailey*, when a trial for a rape was coming on; the Judge suggesting it would produce some very luscious scenes, gave the Ladies intimation, that it would be proper for them to retire, as he was afraid the indelicacy that would assail their ears might put them to the blush; when KITTY arose, and said aloud,—" Well, my Lord, " I don't mind, I'll take my chance."

Miss H——D, whom we have already had occasion to celebrate as Lord DEL—'s Dulcinea, and for whose portrait we refer the Reader to the *Historiette* in which may be found that connexion, frequently appears here. The truth is, since that Nobleman's diftreffes, she has been
compelled

compelled to keep a fharp look-out for
a genteel maintenance; and fhe endeavours to realize fome fmall provifion for
her future days, as fhe is confcious that
her charms are upon the decline, and
that an antiquated Toaft, inftead of being
able to fix a price upon her attractions,
muft, if fhe is willing to give a loofe to
her amorous defires, in turn pay for gratification.

THESE and feveral other Ladies of
the fame difpofition and rank vifit here;
and Mrs. R——DS——N ufually takes
care to cater for the parties, as fhe
judges will be fatisfactory to them
both; though fometimes fhe has been
guilty of an error in judgement (like the
unfortunate BYNG). But though fhe
might receive a volley of oaths from the
male fide, and a blunderbufs of fcolding
and abufe from the Ladies, fhe has always
escaped

efcaped with her life, though not without frequent and fevere mortifications for her errors.

THE D. of A. came here one evening with his party, and having gained admiffion, thought the Ladies were to be compelled to capitulate upon their terms, but they found their miftake, and all retired but one, who judged he could prevail in their abfence with a Mifs L—N, who paffed for a prude, and was thought by many never to have yielded to any man, notwithftanding fhe frequented Mrs. R—DS—N's. He began at firft to rally her pretended mo defty, and faid, he would convince her, there was not any fuch thing as real chaftity amongft the Female World. He faid, he had intimately ftudied the Sex for many years, all their artifices, devices, ftratagems, affectations, hypocrily, hypocrify, and diffimulation. He added, that in order to reafon with precifion upon the fubject, he had with much labour and affiduity formed a fcale of female amorous paffions, and pretended continence, which he propofed laying before the Royal Society, and for which he did not doubt he fhould meet with their thanks and approbation. Saying this, he pulled out a paper, which was intitled,

A

A SCALE OF FEMALE INCONTINENCE AND CONTINENCE.

WE will suppose the highest Degree to be THIRTY-ONE, when the Game is certainly up—*to a Hole*, and the Calculation will be found thus.

1	*Furor Uterinus*	31.	2	in	100
2	One digit below the *Furor*	30.	4	in	100
3	To be completely gratified	29.	6	in	40
4	Extravagant passions	28	10	in	50
5	Insurmountable desires	27.	12	in	60
6	Enchanting pantings	26.	6	in	10
7	Inordinate titillation	25	8	in	30
8	Occasional phrenzies	24	9	in	17
9	Incessant lingerings	23.	5	in	18
10	Violent affections	22.	3	in	12
11	Uncontroulable appetites	21.	6	in	25
12	Salacious itchings	20.	1	in	3
13	Inordinate desires	19	3	in	4
14	Voluptuous sensations	18	1	in	1
15	Untoward, vicious caprices	17	4	in	11
16	Captivating ideas	16.	4	in	5
17	Nocturnal involuntary emissions	15.	2	in	30
18	Disappointed lasses troubled with the Green-sickness	14	1	in	100
19	Self-pollution at boarding schools	13.	12	in	13
20	Perspective fruition	12.	12	all	
21	On the brink of consummation	11.	14	in	15
22	Fatal tardiness	10.	1	in	11
23	Captivating hopes	9.	1	in	2
24	Ripe for enjoyment	8.	all above 14		
25	Youthful proneness	7.	every female at any age		
26	Antedated joys	6.	4	in	5
27	Flattering hopes, and fluttering expectations	5.	3	in	9
28	Temporary lasciviousness	4.	3	in	4
29	Judicious prudery	3.	1	in	20
30	Controulable chastity	2.	4	in	1000
* 31	Cold, frigid insensibility	1.	1	in	100,000

* The Reader will perceive, we have taken this Scale up and down, backwards and forwards, having an eye to *Aretin* in every particular.

You

You fee, Madam, faid *Calculator*, how much the odds are againft you at ftart-ing; and I fuppofe by this time, inftead of one hundred thoufand, it is more than a million to one againft you. In a word, *Calculator* played his part fo well as an Orator, a Lover, and a Calcula-tor, that ere now he had approved him-felf fo juft a candidate to her favour, and to the higheft *digit* of blifs, that fhe fell gently into his arms, and acknow-ledged there was no fupporting the cha-racter of a Prude after there were fo much odds againft her.

THIS Scale of *Incontinence* has carried us a little *figuratively* out of the line we prefcribed to ourfelves; but as the *eloped* CLARA and the beauteous Mrs. W—N are announced, we fhall drop the calcu-lative curtain, and fuppofe that *Calcu-lator* has by this time convinced Mifs

L———N

L——N he is as good a judge of the practical, as the theoretical salacious part of the fair sex; and shall retire to make room for Sir WILLIAM B—, and Lord S—, now under affliction for the loss of his dearest enchantress, and the perplexity of the affairs of *Greenwich Hospital,* and more so for the still greater perplexed sttate of the Nation. The D. of A. is, moreover, expected every hour to return; and for fear of a *Tourbillon,* as it is not impossible Sir HUGH may light up a candle or two here upon his *honourable acquittal,* we shall quit the premises *à la sourdine.*

CHAP.

* C H A P. XLI.

A Portrait of Mrs. MATTHEWS's Nunnery. Some Description of several celebrated Thais's. Lord L———N is introduced: An Outline of his Lordship's Character. His Amours. Acquaintance with the famous, or infamous Mrs. R—DD, through Mrs A—R. An uncommon Conflict, arising from a Fit of Jealousy. Its Consequences. Sketch of the Conduct of Counsellor BAILEY.

WE will now suppose ourselves ushered in at Mrs MATTHEWS's, and introduced to this sagacious Lady, who is deeply read in all the mysteries of her profession. She was sitting with a young *Tit* in the parlour, and giving her instructions how to behave to a rich Jew Merchant, for whom she was provided that evening. Miss

Sм—тн (for that was the name she went by) was about sixteen, was very pretty, and rather appeared the Hoyden than the accomplished young Lady She was dressed in a white frock, and pink sash; and had every mark of youth and innocence. She seemed a good deal terrified on finding she was to be sacrificed to a Jew; and was in a flood of tears at our entrance. To cheer up her spirits, Mis. MATTHEWS had recourse to the Ratafia bottle, and compelled her to drink a large glass. The bottle circulated, and general conversation ensued, when Miss V—nce—t and Miss Ar—ld were introduced. The first of these Ladies had a very good face, was remarkably plump, and appeared to be pregnant, as she afterwards acknowledged. The latter was almost the reverse: she was very delicate, but seemed to be in a decl ne.

WE

WE had not been long in this situation before Lord L—— was announced. His Lordship had just come from the House of Peers, where he had made a flowery speech in defence of Administration, and was so elated at the applause he had met with from the First Commissioner of a certain Board, that he could not refrain from giving us the substance of the harangue, with the approbation he had met with from Lord S——. " By G—d, L——, you have " outdone your usual outdoings !—A De- " mosthenes, a Cicero !— Why, you " knocked them down as flat as a floun- " der—they had not a word to say in " reply R——D was mute, and R—M " was struck dumb Go on, my Boy, and " you may depend upon all possible " encouragement." This, his Lord- ship told us, was the eulogium he had received, which made us call to mind

the

the following lines in *The Diaboliad*, but to whom applied we do not recollect:

Then in succession came a Peer of words,
Well known,—and honour'd in the *House of Lords*,
Whose eloquence all parallel defies;
So SANDWICH says, and SANDWICH never lies.
No doubt, the partial Earl delights to see,
In this young Lord, his own Epitome.

LORD L—'s well-known celebrity for intrigue and dissipation had greatly hurt his fortune; the trees had been lopt, and the dirty acres mortgaged, yet his propensity for women and play still prevailed, and he could not see a handsome female, that was attainable by address or money, without sacrificing every prudential consideration to his passion. Neither could he hear a dice-box rattle in a Chocolate-house, without being stimulated at their enchanting eccho; and though he might that morning have borrowed a hundred at *cent. per cent.* to remove an execution in his house, yet,

for-

forgetting his diftreffes and neceffities, the harmony of *feven is the main* was irrefift-ible; and this bewitching found, like a Syren's voice, bewildered him to part with every guinea. Can it then be afto-nifhing, that his Lordfhip fhould be in-ceffantly tormented for money, efpeci-ally when it is confidered, that the ex-travagant Mrs. A——R is upon the lift of his miftreffes; and that the famous, or infamous Mrs. R—DD is her conftant confidante ánd companion ? What re-fource is then left for him? He muft roar in the Senate againft minifterial malverfation, to be bought off with a place or penfion. That he has oratori-cal talents cannot be difputed. Nature had been very bountiful to him in be-ftowing on him fuch mental talents, as could not fail fhining, with the educa-tion he has received · His voice was harmonious, his perfon tall and genteel, and his action graceful. Add to thefe

M 3

quali-

qualifications, he had a tenacious memory, and was poffeffed of that happy effrontery which fecures a man from the fhafts of raillery, or the confufion of an abrupt or unexpected replication. With thefe rudiments of eloquence, it will not be doubted, that he made a mafterly figure in moft debates of importance. In a word, he was too formidable an adverfary for Adminiftration not to liften to. They knew his diftrefs. Cerberus muft have a fop to prevent his barking, at leaft on that fide of the queftion. A bargain was ftruck, and how eafy the tranfition! He immediately perceived his error! A fett of men, who aimed at the deftruction of their Country, and aimed the poignard of nefarious malverfation at her very vitals, inftantly appeared to him fenfible, upright, judicious, immaculate Minifters. We are all liable to error, but we are not all fo capable

pable of difcovering our miftakes with fuch a ready eye, and acknowledging our faults *.

THIS fketch will fufficiently convey an idea of the Noble Peer here introduced. Mrs. A—R having gained intelligence from a trufty chairman, whom fhe employed as a Myrmidon to watch the actions of Lord L———, that he had repaired to MATTHEWS's, after having waited dinner for him near three hours; upon the wings of jealoufy flew to *King's-Place*, accompanied by Mrs. R—DD, and Counfellor BAILEY, her former advocate and prefent great admirer. Having gained admittance, a moft violent fcene enfued. Mrs. A—R inftantly fell foul of Mrs. MATTHEWS, and a warm action en-

---

* Lord L———N's la e defection is accounted for, by being refufed the fuccefforfhip of Lord SUFFOLK, as Secretary of State for the Northern department.

fued,

fued, not without high heads flying about, and bald heads being displayed. Every one now interfered to part the combatants, but in this attempt, the Counfellor, who was, as ufual, very much intoxicated, was undefignedly knocked down, and received a bloody nofe from Mrs. A—r. At length peace was reftored, except in words, which were ftill vociferated by this laft Lady, in all the *Billingfgate* that her fancy could fupply.

LORD L—— thought it was his turn to fpeak, and, in a flowery oration, (thinking he was ftill in a certain Affembly, where Mrs A—r's language is often introduced) framed an apology to the Lady of the houfe for the confufion his vifit had occafioned, and affured her that reparation fhould be made for any damage Mrs. MATTHEWS's head or clothes might have fuftained. After this, the Counfel-

lor's

lor's face being washed, the blood being previously wiped away, the belligerent party returned peaceably in the coach which had brought them, but not without having taken his Lordship in tow.

HAVING introduced Counsellor BAILEY, the Reader may not be displeased with the sketch of so extraordinary a character. This gentleman was a native of Ireland, and came over here about fifteen years ago, to enter as a Student in the Middle Temple, and after the proper time was admitted at the Bar. It cannot be said he made any capital figure here, but was chiefly employed at Hicks's-Hall and the Old-Bailey. He had a small patrimony, upon which he lived for some time in a genteel manner, but falling into company with sharpers, they soon stripped him of all his little fortune. This irreparable loss hurried him into a series of debaucheries,

baucheries, which hurt his conftitution, and brought him to fo debilitated a ftate, as to be incapable, at times, of croffing the ftreet. An inftance of this happened fome time fince, when he fell down, and was run over by the wheel of a coach, which endangered his life, and it was fome months before he recovered from the bruifes he received.

WHEN the celebrated trial of Mrs. R—DD came on at the Old-Bailey, he was employed as her Counfel; and tho' he was of no kind of fervice to her, the fees he demanded were very confiderable; and as fhe at that time was much reduced, and could not afford to pay him in fpecie, he agreed to fettle the account by her transferring her perfon to him. They accordingly lived together for fome time, but being of a jealous difpofition, and fancying fhe gave the preference to a rival, he, he in an act of

defperation, cut his throat, tho' not in a
manner to render the wound mortal.
This affair created a rupture between
them, and having no longer the run of
her table, or Lord L——'s kitchen,
his diftreffes became very great, all his
wearing apparel, except a thread-bare
coat, was foon difpofed of, and, to clofe
his miferable end, he was obliged to
take refuge in a Work-houfe, where he
terminated his mortal career a fhort
time fince. Let this ferve as a leffon to
the gay and extravagant Bucks, Bloods,
and Macaronies of the Age, who fquan-
der their fortunes in brothels with
wh—es and gamblers! Let them have the
unfortunate Counfellor BAILEY before
their eyes every time they are going to
commit an act of extravagancy, and re-
member there are more work-houfes
than that of *St. Martin's in the Fields*.

CHAP.

*C H A P. XLII.

Sketch of KITTY FR—D—R—CK's *Life.
Her false Ambition displayed* KITTY
*consents to an Interview with the Duke
of* —— *at Mrs.* MATTHEWS's. *A
Half-Length of a graceless Grace, from a
celebrated Poem.*— *Another Half-Length,
by way of Drapery, in Prose, to complete
the Portrait, and give it in full. A curious genuine Dialogue between a gam-
bling Nobleman and his Taylor.*

THE celebrated KITTY F—D—RICK
is a Lady so well known, as being
classed among the Thais's of the *Haut
Ton*, that to mention her name is almost
sufficient to depict her at full length to
our Readers, but lest some of them
should not be so well acquainted with
her

her as might be imagined, we fhall give a little fketch of her likenefs, which may be feen in almoft all the Print-fhops. KITTY was the daughter of an induftrious tradefman, and being an only child, was, as ufual, her mother's pet. This darling was confidered as a moft beautiful girl; it is true, fhe had many attractions, and might be pronounced tolerably pretty. Her doating parents thinking fhe was entitled to make her fortune, and ride in her coach, on this piefumption gave her an education fuited to that rank which they fancied fhe would move in. To a boarding-fchool of eminence fhe was accordingly fent, and there taught mufic, French, and dancing. Her natuial vanity being much inflated by the example and opinions of her fchool-fellows, who talked of nothing but Peers and Coronets, fhe

VOL. II.   K   began

began to think she was as much entitled
to this rank as any of them, and accordingly, upon her return from school,
she refused some offers that were made
her of marriage, judging they were unworthy of being accepted, though, in
fact, they were beyond what in her station
of life she could reasonably expect. One
of her suitors was a Factor of some opulence, and another a young gentleman
who had great expectations of being admitted a partner in a capital bankinghouse.

KITTY now frequented *Ranelagh* and
the *Pantheon*, and soon attracted the attention of many Noblemen, who found
it no difficult matter to be introduced to
her; and the civil things they said,
consummate vanity made her construe into a declaration of a real and

honourable

honourable paſſion. Lord P—— at length prevailed, and ſhe gave up her honour to a Peer, rather than ſubmit to be the wife of an eminent Citizen. Amazing infatuation! and the more ſo, when we conſider that his Lordſhip was married, and could not poſſibly offer her his hand in a conjugal way. But there is a ſtrange ambition implanted in the ſex, and many of them carry the frenzy ſo far, as to think it more eligible to be the wh——e of a Lord, than the wife of a Commoner.

AFTER a few weeks his Lordſhip left her, and KITTY now began to ruminate upon her folly, but it was too late to recede, for even her parents, who had been originally inſtrumental in putting ridiculous notions into her head of pomp and grandeur, upon this firſt *faux pas*, forſook her. In this ſituation,

ſhe

she was compelled to put her charms to sale to the best bidder, and a variety of Enamoratos succeeded. Her heart was full perfectly disengaged, the first sacrifice she had made to vanity and false ambition—the succeeding arose entirely from necessity. However, at length, she met with an amiable young gentleman named Mr. F—k; his person was very agreeable and genteel, his sentiments noble and generous, and his ideas seemed to belpeak him descended of a royal race. It is said, that he was grandson of the late Theodore King of Corsica, and that he was not without hopes of one day succeeding to his grandsire's throne. This consideration, though very chimerical, might perhaps have had some influence upon KITTY's heart, and possibly stimulated her ambition to soar at regal dignity, especially as he suffered her to go by his name, and many con-
jectured

jectured they were really married. Be
this as it may, it is certain Mr F—k
was the only man who had made any
impreffion upon her affections, and
there continued for a confiderable time
a very tender and affectionate correfpondence, till at length, he having received a Commiffion in the Army, was
ordered with his regiment to America,
where foon after, in an engagement with
the American army, after acquitting
himfelf with great courage and intrepi-
dity, he fell upon the field of battle,
greatly lamented by all his friends and
acquaintance; but by none more than
KITTY, who, upon hearing the melancholy news, put on widow's weeds,—but
her external forrow was far furpaffed by
her inward feelings.

THIS Lady had many offers made
her of connexions and fettlements, her

admirers

admirers having hitherto confidered Mr F—k as an infuperable obftacle to the fole poffeffion either of her affections or her perfon, and therefore had refrained from making thefe overtures till this period.

Amongst the number of her adulators was a certain Duke, who had it not before in his power to make her a fettlement, his finances being, till his late fucceffion, in a very embarraffed ftate, but now having come to an ample fortune, as well as a Ducal title, he applied to Mis Matthews to invite Mifs F——k to an interview at her houfe; and as the propofal entirely fuited her difpofition, coming from a man of his Grace's rank, and who had fo confpicuoufly diftinguifhed himfelf in the Republic of Gallantry, fhe readily obeyed the mandate.

THAT

THAT the Reader may form a juft idea of the perfon, qualities, and difpofition of this Nobleman, we think the following quotation from a poem publifhed fome time fince, may be here properly introduced.

With eafy meafur'd fteps, lo! * appears,
And ftrives to hide the wafte of wrinkling years.
Time had long wafh'd the bloom from off his face,
But the enliv'ning rouge fupplies the place
Through the large circle of near half an age, ⎫
This Lord has ftrutted on the public ftage, ⎬
The foppifh Prince of Fops, the Macaroni Sage. ⎭
But, charm'd with trifles, pleas'd with every toy,
Still he is young,—*if Folly makes the Boy*
The verdant Ribbon grac'd his filken veft,
The Star's pale filver glitter'd on his breaft;
While, to a nearer ken, his wrinkles fhew
The furrow'd emblems of the batter'd Beau.
At fam'd Newmarket he was taught to cheat,
To league with Grooms, and frame th' unerring
            Bett,
Here learn'd the Jockey's Art—and, what is worfe,
Practis'd the Jockey's Arts upon the Courfe

SUCH

SUCH is the picture drawn of his gracelefs Grace by the Author of the *Diaboliad*; and we think the following fcene in *Piccadilly*, which, we are affured, is genuine, will give his Lordfhip's Poitrait at full length.

LORD PICCADILLY, (*as he was then called*) *yawning*.

What a damned run of luck laft night!—The devil furely got into the bones, for they would not operate.—If I could have cogged that laft caft, I fhould have brought myfelf home, and been five hundied in pocket; but Sir HARRY has an hawk's eye, and 'tis impoffible almoft to do it with him undetected !

Enter a Servant.

SER. My Lord, Mr. BUCKRAM is below.

LORD.

LORD P. Why, there let him remain --if you can't turn him out - How often, you rafcal, have I told you, that I never was at home, but when he brought a new fuit of clothes?

SER. Why, my Lord, that is exactly the cafe, or, your Lordfhip may depend upon it, I fhould not have admitted him over the threfhold.

LORD P. *O! fi c'eft comme cela à la bon heur.* Shew him up—I was fo enveloped in the thought of laft night's d—n'd ill run, that I had entirely forgot I had ordered this fuit.

[Re-enter Servant, with Mr. BUCKRAM, who exhibits a new fuit au dernier goût]

BUCK. I have the honour to wait upon your Lordfhip, with, I think, one
of

of the moſt elegant ſuits that an Engliſh Nobleman ever wore,—all French,
I aſſure your Lordſhip, trimmings and
all.

LORD P—. Very right, BUCKRAM—
or do you think I would have wore it
elſe.

[*Puts it on, and admires himſelf in a French
plate-glaſs that reaches from the ceiling
to the ground, and in the* vis-a-vis *pannel there is another of the ſame manufacture and dimenſions*]

LORD P——. I think it will do.—
Yes, I think with very little alteration
it may do.

BUCK. To a charm, my Lord.

LORD.

LORD P. This cuff, I think, let me look again, is not *affez badinant*.

BUCK. Oh! pofitively, my Lord, never was a finer cut.—It was done by my foreman, who is a Parifian, and was efteemed at *Verfailles* as a very great operator.

LORD P. Are you fure of that?—Well then, it may be paffable, it will do. —You need not wait, BUCKRAM--I fhall fend to you next week, as foon as I have fixed upon another pattern.

BUCK. I beg your Lordfhip ten thoufand pardons, and hope your Lord-fhip will not be offended at my prefent-ing my bill.

LORD P. Oh no!—(*looks at the bill*) I fee the total is feventeen hundred and

fome

fome odd pounds.—I fuppofe it is right caft up—I know you are pretty exact.

Buck. Yes, my Lord, you will fee it is very right, if your Lordfhip compares it with the bill I had the honour to prefent your Lordfhip laft year.

Lord P. I never keep fuch things by me, much lefs in my head—fo I fhall give myfelf no farther trouble about it.

Buck. I am forry, my Lord, to be obliged to remind your Lordfhip, that at this time of year we tradefmen are in great want of money.

Lord P. And, egad, we Noblemen are in as great want of it, all the year round.

Buck.

BUCK. Yes, my Lord, but our drapers and mercers ——

LORD P. What, do they play deep? —If they do, you may introduce them. You shall go with me, and I shall be able to bring you home.

BUCK. Oh! no, my Lord, they never play for a farthing—it is all in the way of trade.

LORD P. Then it is not a debt of honour you are troubled about?—*Bagatelle donc, foutaise.*

BUCK. If your Lordship could not let me have the whole, I should be much obliged to your Lordship for part.

LORD P. Part, BUCKRAM!--No—no, take the whole, (*returns him the bill*) and never let me fee it again—I hate doing things by halves.

BUCK. But I hope your Lordfhip will have fome compaffion.—You know your Lordfhip promifed me laft year, but I can't fay, with humble fubmiffion, that your Lordfhip was fo good as your word —You know, my Lord, a Peer's honour fhould be facred, as it goes as far as another man's oath.

LORD P. Why, you blockhead, if I could not pay you when it was fo much lefs —how the devil do you think I can pay you now, when it is much more? But, to be ferious—I've had a damn'd ill run of luck lately; and even laft night, after I was obliged to pay a capital

tal Debt of Honour, I was ftript of
every remaining farthing, and I could
now as foon raife the dead as five pounds,
unlefs PAPILLOT can furnifh me with
fome cafh, for my credit is exhaufted at
ARTHUR's, and BOB would as foon truft
Buckhorfe as me with a fingle Rouleau.
--But I can afford you fome hopes.—I've
three horfes to ftart on Tuefday at Newmarket—a dead hollow thing—a regular
plant—I muft clear a thoufand at leaft.
—There, you fee, is an excellent chance
for you! Many a man has gone into the
Acre, and ordered a chariot upon the
ftrength of a worfe. But more immediate comfort for you, befides this, I have
a little private *hazard* here to-night,
with a Welfh Baronet, as rich as a Na-
bob, and as flat as a flounder ——I certainly fhall have him at the beft—and,
by G—d, and upon my Honour (*which*

is much more) you fhall fairly go with the cafter.

BUCKRAM finding it impoffible to fqueeze a guinea out of his Lordfhip at this crifis, judged it prudent to retire; and eventually very judicioufly, for the Welch Baronet having *bled freely* that night, Lord PICCADILLY fent BUCK-RAM two hundred the next day.

CHAP.

C H A P. XXXV.

The Terms on which KITTY accepts his Grace's Proposals. A comparative View, in the Morning, between the amorous Powers of the Young King of Corsica (Elect) and the Duke of ——. A Transition from a splendid House, elegantly furnished for KITTY, and the lamentable Situation of Miss N—LS—N. A whimsical Distress, which is prefaced by a genuine Anecdote of Captain TOPER. The lucky Sequel.

THE Reader has been, for some short time, diverted from the result of the interview at Mrs MATTHEWS's, between the Duke of —— and KITTY F——K. After some few compliments on both sides, his Grace said to her,

"My

" My dear KITTY, it is now in my
" power to make a decent provision for
" you, and it was for that reafon that I
" defired Mrs MATTHEWS to invite you
" to this *tête-à-tête*.   I will now be very
" explicit, and tell you my propofals .
" I will fettle a hundred a-year upon
" you for life; furnifh you a genteel
" houfe , allow you ten guineas a-week
" for its main enance , and keep you a
" carriage." She nodded acquiefcence,
and he prefented her, as a pledge of
his honour, a bill of a hundred
pounds. Supper was now ordered, and
after a fumptuous repaft they retired to
reft, where we fhall leave them for a few
hours, to give a full loofe to their amorous appetites, after having laid in a
flock of abilties, in the moft falacious
viands, and the moft generous wines.

RISING

Rising in the morning, Kitty happened to meet with the Poem of the *Torpedo* upon the toilette, left there the day before by some curious, researching Nun; and when she came to the following lines, burst out into such a loud laugh, that his Grace, who was not yet *risen*, cried out, "What the Devil, "Kate, is come to you?"—"Nothing at all, my Lord; but this pas- "sage is enough to tickle any woman's "fancy, who has been a-bed all night "with a half-worn-out Debauchee!— "Not that I mean your Grace—but "only hear.

"What though to give F—tzp—tr—ck fire,
"May no celestial art require,
　"For he can catch like tinder.
"Have I not rais'd a doubt of flame
'In M—ch's wither'd, feeble frame,
　"Though burnt before to cinder?"

"Well

" WELL said his Grace), and where
" the Devil is the joke?—I can't find
" it *out*" " No, my Lord (replied she)
" and what is worse—I could not find
" it *in*." " A truce with your jokes,
" KITTY, my reputation for Gallantry
" has been *too long* established to be now
" called in question" " *Too long*, in-
" deed (rejoined KITTY), in every
" sense:—it is *so long* established, that
" it is now become as flimsy as boiled
" tripe."

His Grace turned on the other side,
and snored out a reply, as he did not
much admire the disquisition, whilst
KITTY, after reading out the Poem, began to consider the comparative differ-
ence between the young King Elect,
and the old Peer Erect; and after a
few minutes reverie, pronounced to
herself in French: " *Ce n'est pas la lon-*
" *gueur,*

" *gueur ni la largeur des chofes qui fait*
" *leur merit* Priape *furanné ne vaut*
" *pas* Hercule *à vingt ans.*"

THAT the mere Englifh Reader may underftand us, I mean KITTY, we fhall give a literal tranflation. " It is not " the length or circumference of " things that conftitutes their merit :— " *Priapus* fuperannuated, is not equal " to *Hercules* at twenty."

HOWEVER, notwithftanding this opinion, which, if the Reader fhould happen to be a Female, and of any experience in the Cytherean Rites, fhe will certainly affent to; the terms offered by his Grace were fuch as, fhe thought, prudence dictated for her to accept. Accordingly, at breakfaft fhe changed her tone, and inftead of laughing *with* the Author of the *Torpedo*, fhe

now

now pretended to laugh *at* him, saying it was a stupid, insipid, balderdash performance, a mere catchpenny, penned by some poor devil of a Garretteer to get a dinner. His Grace was pleased with the determination, for he had read the Poem before, and was greatly mortified to see himself so justly pourtrayed, and upon KITTY's saying, she thought his Grace was a Nobleman of the greatest *Parts* of any one in England, and in which she was no false voucher, he threw another Bank-note of a hundred pounds into her lap, saying, he hoped she would not, like FANNY MURRAY, pretend she could not make a breakfast of it *

His

---

* The Anecdote which has generally prevailed upon this subject is as follows. When FANNY lived with Sir RICHARD ATKINS, she one morning, at breakfast, was very urgent for money to pay a Jeweller,

His Grace, upon his return home, ordered his two Valet and Mercury to look out for a genteel house, about sixty pounds a year, in the New Buildings, and he having fixed upon one suitable to the design, his Grace gave orders to the Upholsterer to furnish the house in a proper manner.

Having now fixed Kitty in her new house, after taking a house-warming with her, we shall leave her to reflect upon her good fortune, and gratify her vanity and ambition, in being the Duchess of ———, Elect.

---

a Jeweller, and upon Sir Richard's procuring a bank-note, and declaring that was all he had in the world, she put it between two slices of bread and butter, and after eating it (bread and butter fashion), said it was not sufficient to make a breakfast of.

Ler

LET not, however, the Reader imagine, that every female who devoted her charms a facrifice to promifcuous proftitution, was as fortunate as KITTY FRED—K. To evince this affertion, we fhall prefent our Readers with a fcene in real life. The Reader has, in the preceding Volume, been introduced to Mifs N—LSON, and made acquainted with her religious difafter, in purfuit of Lady CR—VEN's Tea pot:—we fhall now pay this Lady another vifit, in order to enquire how far her *pious endeavours* have been crowned with fuccefs, after having received thofe religious and neceffary inftructions from her friend and paramour the Jefuit.

MISS N—LSON had been feveral times at the S———n Chapel, and had played off all the artillery of her ogles upon his Excellency; and fhe more than once
flattered

flattered herself with a favourable effect; but she had never yet had an opportunity of engaging in an interview with him. To-night there was a Masquerade at the *Pantheon*, and she was informed, from good authority, that the Ambassador would be present. Accordingly she resolved to go, let what would happen. Drunken Captain TOPER had called upon her that forenoon, and at the sight of him, she had the most sanguine expectations of being presented with a ticket,—but alas! the Captain was quite broke down—he had not a guinea in the world; and he was curfing his ill-natured stars for being thus destitute of cash, at a time when a Masquerade was going forward— an amusement that he could no more refrain from (if the *Mopus's*, as he called them, were aboard) than he could refrain from the Burgundy and Champaign, when once he had got in. The Captain had got drunk upon the ftrength of the difappointment, and in going home to his lodgings, in *Rathbone-Place*, bred fuch a riot as convened a numerous mob before his own door; and it was neceffary to fend for Peace-officers, to prevent the outrages of the populace, who had taken it into their heads that Vice Admiral P—ll—ser had taken refuge there.

Such being Mifs Nels—n's difappointment, there was but one refource left, which was to difpatch her maid to the Pawnbroker's with her beft facque and petticoat, her black filk jacket and coat, and even her laft Devonfhire brown; but all thefe together produced no more than a fufficient fum to purchafe a ticket. What was to be done? A thought was as rapid as the diftrefs was great. The watch at the bed head, a fixture that went with the apartment, immediately struck her, and directly it was conveyed to My Uncle's by her maid. Indeed, though a *nominal fixture*, had it been wound up, and put at the threshold of the street-door, it had been the road so often, that it would have found the way of itself, without a conductor or regulator. But unfortunately, even this, which was considered as a *dernière resource*, would not do—it produced but fifteen shillings, and half a guinea more was at least requisite. Another expedient was absolutely necessary. Poor N—lson's whole wardrobe consisted at present of three smocks, and what was upon her back. They were presently bundled up, and transmitted to her Relation's; and she was now, literally, reduced to her last shift.

THIS,

This, the Reader will fay, was a bold ftroke for a Lover, but the die was caft, and fhe could not now recede. To the Mafquerade fhe repaired in a Shepherdefs's drefs, which greatly became her. The Ambaffador was ftruck with the elegance and beauty of her figure, fingled her out, and walked a minuet with her, taking N—lson for a Woman of Fafhion, as fhe did not affociate with any of the Nunnery Grizettes, whom fhe ftudioufly avoided. The confequence was, he waited upon her home, remained till morning, and made her a prefent by far more than fufficient to bring home her *effects*, and pay what arrears of rent fhe owed. Upon his retiring, he promifed to renew his vifits in a few days, fo well pleafed was he with the reception he had met with.

CHAP.

C H A P XXXVI.

A Trip to Berkeley-Street. Amours of Lord G——r. Attachment of the M——ly——ts (Father and Son), as referred to in The Diaboliad. Lord G——r's Improvement upon GALE's Elastic Beds. The great Skill of Mrs. W——st——n's Riding-Masters. Description and Characters of Mrs W——st——n's Female Visitors. The Three Graces introduced, in the Persons of Miss C——rter, Miss St——nley, and Miss Armstr——ng, with some striking Anecdotes of their Lives.

WE think it may not be amiss now to take a trip to *Berkeley-Street, Piccadilly*, as we there shall find a celebrated Lady Abbess under the name of Mrs. W--st--n. This Lady is

L 3

sister

fifter to the head Groom and chief Pimp of Lord Gro--ner. Her brother firft put her upon this plan, and at the fame time infured her his Lordfhip's cuftom, protection, and recommendation; and in this refpect he has fully compleated his promife;—for though his Lordfhip may fometimes wander in the purlieus of *King's-Place*, or the environs of *Mary-bone*, his chief attraction is in *Berkeley-Street*. Here he conftantly meets Mifs Hayw—d twice a-week, and fometimes oftener.

No Duenna upon the *Ton* underftands bufinefs better than Mrs W—st—n. She has Nuns of every fize and complexion at her nod, though only two live in the houfe—Louisa Sm—th and Carolina J—nes. The former of thefe is alternately vifited by the M—ly—ts*,

M.—LY—TS*, Father and Son; and as she considers it *all in the Family-way*, she would think it, according to Mr. WILKES, entirely orthodox, if a third person of the same breed were introduced. Old M—LY—T, who now verges upon sixty, is still a Rake at heart, and after having debauched more women than, perhaps, any man in the course of this century—being quite tired of S——F, and satiated with M——X, thinks LOUISA an excellent Piece, tho' rivalled by his own son, *natural indeed*, who is supported, through the agency of Miss SM—TH, by his father's bounty.

THIS Lady no sooner heard that CHARLOTTE HAYES had retired from

---

* Vide The DIABOLIAD, in the Note, p. 13.

L 4   business.

bufinefs, than fhe immediately applied to her, and purchafed all her *Elaſtic Beds*, invented by that great creative genius Count O'K——LY, and conſtructed by that celebrated mechanic and upholſter- er Mr. GALE. Not fatisfied, however, with being in poffeſſion of thefe *Elaſtic Beds*, which give the fineſt movements in the moſt extatic moments, with- out trouble or the leaſt fatigue to ther Agent or Patient, fhe requeſted Lord GRO——NER (who has alfo a fine *mechanical* genius, and has already made a great improvement upon Mrs. PHIL- LIPS's *Machines*, by fecuring them in fuch a manner that they can never break in action) to throw out fome hints for the improvement of thefe *Elaſtic Beds*, and he immediately conceived an additional fpring, to the amazing grati- fication and fenfation of the Actor and Actrefs, as CLARÁ HAYW——D can well teſtify.

teſtify. To this additional ſpring we may, in a great meaſure, aſcribe the uncommon vogue that Mrs. W--ST--N's houſe is now in, being frequented by Peers and Peereſſes, Wanton Wives, and more Wanton Widows; ſhe having at the ſame time, in conſtant pay, ſome of the moſt capital *Riding-Maſters** in the Three Kingdoms, always ready to mount at a minute's warning, who can either walk, trot, or gallop, as is moſt agreeable to their female pupils.

HITHER alſo reſort many Thais's upon the *Ton*, whoſe neceſſities compel them to accept of pecuniary rewards; among theſe are Miſs S—BR—K, from *Newman-Street*. This Lady is the daughter of a Broker, who reſided in *Round-Court* near the *Strand*. She is a

---

* Stallions, alias Petticoat-Penſioners.

L 5 ſine

fine fair girl, with a dark-expreffive eye, and good brown hair: She is about the middle fize, very genteel, and recommends ftill more the elegance of her perfon by the magnificence of her drefs. She is in *nominal* keeping by Captain B—y; but it is fcarce poffible, that the Captain's pay (and as to fortune we never could learn that he poffeffed any) can fupport himfelf and Mifs S—BR—K in the fumptuous manner fhe appears. The enigma is better folved by her frequent vifits to Mrs. W—ST—N, where Lord I——M and fome other Noblemen often toaft her. Mifs D—S—N of *Sadler's-Wells* fometimes makes her exhibition here; but this is only when fhe is fent for as a good crummy Piece who fings a good fong, as the expence of coach-hire from *Cold-Bath-Fields* muft to a certainty be de-frayed,

frayed, before she can think of making this excursion; more especially as her last benefit was on a wet night, and of course she had but a thin house. Colonel F—TZ—Y, as master of the Revels here, presides upon this occasion, and Miss D—W—N affords him such gratification as surpasses even Twelfth Night. Miss R——YN——DS, another Lady from *Newman-Street*, frequently makes her appearance at Mrs. W—ST—N's. She is tall and genteel, her features very delicate, her hair inclined to the classic tinge. We may also reckon Miss C—R—TER, Miss ST—NLEY and Miss A—M—ST—G among the visitors of this Seminary. These Ladies are so well known upon the *Haut Ton*, and their persons are so perfectly described at the Print-shops, that we think it needless to dwell upon their charms, or delineate their portraits.

THE firſt of theſe Ladies was ſome time ſince in keeping by Sir William D——; but detecting her in the amorous embraces of his Valet-de-Chambre, he literally kicked her out of doors. She, however, ſoon got acquainted with Lord B——, and it was his Lordſhip who put her upon ſo elegant a footing, as to make the Painters and Deſigners take particular notice of her, and exhibit her pretty face in public. She has a ſneaking fondneſs for Captain L——; but as the luſt of money is the greateſt *luſt* that actuates all her conduct, and as the Captain is rather ſeedy, ſhe occaſionally plies at Mrs. W—ST—N's, who never fails putting five guineas into her pocket before her departure.

MISS ST——NLEY is a young Lady whoſe pretenſions in life were far ſuperior to the line ſhe now moves in. Her father

father was a very eminent Packer in the City, and she was spoken of as a fortune of ten thousand pounds. After she had received a very polite boarding-school education, she was pronounced one of the most accomplished young Ladies in all *Farringdon Ward*. She received the addresses of several young Gentlemen, many of opulence, but her heart was fixed upon a man of rank, allied to a Noble Family, and who was upon the point of going abroad in a public character. His intentions were honourable, and the day of their nuptials was fixed upon, when, at this very critical juncture, the failure of a capital house in the City, occasioned by the present unfortunate war in America, involved Mr. St——nly in the like calamity. No sooner did his name appear in the Gazette, than Miss St——nly's intended bridegroom

bridegroom difcontinued his vifits, and
fhe heard no more of him, till fhe read
in the papers of his arrival and reception at a certain Foreign Court. Thus
were all her hopes of felicity blafted—
defperation was the only profpect before
her, and in an act of this nature fhe facrificed herfelf to M——z the Jew,
through the mediation of CHARLOTTE
H—YES, for a mere trinket.

Mifs ARMSTR——NG, the laft of this
Trio, whom we may with propriety ftile
the Graces, is a young Lady of uncommon talents, for, befides the charms of
her perfon, which are far fuperior to
what fall to the lot of moft females, fhe
poffeffes an uncommon fhare of underftanding, that has been greatly improved by reading, which, aided by a
very tenacious memory, affords her ma-

ny opportunities of shining upon most subjects. She has a great share of vivacity, and may justly lay claim to a readiness of fancy, a quickness of imagination, a facility of delivery, as would do credit to many who are ranked upon the list of the *Beaux Esprits* of the Age. GEORGE S—LW—N calls her his Sappho, and she has by times been christened by the names of all the Nine Mufes. She possesses so much sense, as to be conscious that her present line of life is truly contemptible, and she only waits for an opportunity of throwing off the shackles of Prostitution. She has some thoughts of going upon the stage, and was actually under the tuition of Mr. GARRICK at the time of his demise, who gave her the most flattering hopes of success in her dramatic career. His loss, which all the admirers of Melpo-

mene

mene and Thalia muſt woefully lament, was a very ſenſible one to Miſs Armst—ng; as in him ſhe loſt her patron, her tutor, and her friend.—When we uſe the laſt word, we do not mean to apply it in an amorous ſenſe, but according to its literal meaning. Neceſſity at preſent compels her to viſit Mrs. W—st—n, and her company is here eagerly ſought for, not ſo much on account of the ſenſual pleaſures ſhe can beſtow, as for her converſation, and the lively turn that ariſes in company from her wonted hilarity and uncommon pleaſantry. She often receives a handſome compliment, without having granted the ſmalleſt favour, except it be that of highly entertaining the gueſts But let it not be imagined that ſhe is deficient in perſonal attractions.—this is far from being the caſe, and if the Reader ſhould

entertain

entertain the smallest doubt of this asseveration, he is referred to the Print-shop in *May's-Buildings*, where he will find a very striking likeness of Miss ARMSTR—NG.

CHAP.

CHAP. XXXVII.

The Medley Chapter, or Rhapsody; in which may be found a Variety of whimsical Facts, Flashes, and Fancies, suited to most Tastes and Dispositions; unexpected Transitions from the Jocular to the Serious, and from the Grave to the Lively; with some Thoughts on Adultery, the Custom of the Turks upon this Occasion; and an Expedient proposed to prevent it here.

WHILST Lady V---E is taking a microscopic view of his Lordship's Sensitive Plant, and with the assistance of this visual magnifier can scarcely perceive a protuberance of one digit, whilst the salacious MESSALINA of the Stable-yard is provoking titillation by the interior use of the elastic

Chinese

Chinese balls, and forces the General to take Cantharides to keep time to her throbs; whilst Lady L—R is learning the *Manege à la St. George* with her Groom, to recover her skill in *horse-womanship*, after her late temporary retreat from the gay world, whilst Lady GRO——R is preparing the new-invented *Cyprian Fly-caps*, first introduced by the *Bird of Paradise* at Mrs PENDERGAST'S *Bal d'Amour*; whilst Lady P——CY is planning a new intrigue with *Le Cocq du Village* of *Hampton*, who has completely established his character with Virgins, Wives and Widows; the globe still revolves upon its own axis; about the equinoxes the days and nights are nearly of the same duration; Senators squabble for the loaves and fishes, the *Outs* attack the *Ins* for malversation in office, and the latter, when they are hard run, have recourse to the previous

vious queſtion, and ſo terminate the debate by a well-ſecured majority.

Such was the preciſe ſtate of affairs upon our entrance on this 37th Chapter of the NOCTURNAL REVELS; a book that we doubt not will be read in every quarter of the globe, by perſons of all religions, perſuaſions, parties and genders, the *Epicene* not excluded, and tranſlated into all the dead and living languages that ever were thought of, penned or invented, that of the Iſland of Formoſa not excepted, though it never exiſted but in the brain of Pſalmanazar. But methinks I hear the ſnarling Critic ſay---" The vanity of ſcrib-
" blers is inſuperable ! Of what utility
" can ſuch a production as this be to the
" World ? What moral can be derived
" from a performance, whoſe ſole de-
" ſign is the exhibition of ſcenes of
" laſciviouſneſs and complicated debau-
" chery ?"

" chery?" To this we *modeftly* anfwer,
It may be the means, by fuch bold,
natural, and genuine portraits, of deter-
ring the innocent and ignorant part of
our fex from purfuing a libertine and
vicious plan of life, when they fee it
enveloped in fo many fatal embarraff-
ments and dangerous fituations · to the
other fex it may point out, through a
juft and faithful medium, the portraits
of their imperial Lords and Mafters,
the Philofophers, Moralifts, and Re-
formers of the age; it will unmafk
and bring forth to view the latent Hypo-
crite, the abandoned married Libertine,
the infamous Preacher, the contemptible Lord, and the fuperftitious Scoun-
drel ---Let the World view thefe mif-
creants in open day, in the full blaze
of the fun, and if fome happy confequences may not be derived, even in a
moral fenfe, from fuch an expofition,

it

it will be the Readers fault, and not
ours. We fhall not in this place enter
any farther into an apology for the
publication of this work, as we have
already touched upon it in more places
than one, but fhall leave the fnarling
Critic to chew the cud of his own fple-
netic cavils, and for a moment take a
view of the mifconduct and indifcretions
of the youthful part of the fair fex who
are efteemed chafte and virtuous, and
who, neverthelefs, are guilty of many
enormities, that certainly, in a moral
fenfe at leaft, bring them upon a level,
if not beneath common proftitution.

How whimfical a tranfition! will
the Reader fay, from a motley kind
of moral Apology to the *Bijoux Indif-
crets* ---*Indifcreet Toys* indeed! which,
neverthelefs, are vended at moft of the
capital Toy fhops in the purlieus of St
James's. To thefe baubles may we
afcribe,

afcribe, in a great meafure, the fatal effects of a Female Boarding-School Education, and which pioduce as many dangerous confequences among the female world, as mafturbation in Boarding Schools for the male fex. Various inftances of their ufe might be produced amongft the juvenile part of the fair fex in high life; and to this caufe may be afcribed the want of many an heir to fome of the firft fucceffions in England. We are told by feveral Authors of well-known veracity, of the fatal effects of thefe practices, and that in fome inftances, the violent exercife of felf-pollution has fo diftorted their bodies, as to render their fex doubtful, and ever after debar them from the embraces of the male fex.

NEVERTHELESS the Reader might be inclined to doubt the authority of thefe writers, and fancy that the *Bijoux Indif-*
crets

crets were only imaginary toys, and that the female fex, fo far from giving way to fuch unnatural practices, revelled at large in the arms of every fine fellow they met, as a certain Nobleman has lately, upon the introduction of an Act of Parliament to "prevent Adultery," declared, That more divorces have taken place during this reign (notwithstanding the exemplary virtue and attachment of a certain royal and illustrious Pair), than the annals of hiftory can produce fince the eftablifhment of empire in thefe kingdoms. But a moment's confideration muft convince him, that the affeverations of the Authors alluded to do not thereby fall to the ground. We are well apprized, that when once the real and natural *Senfitive Plant* has had its due influence, and been enjoyed in its full bloom and perfection, that thefe factitious Emblems of Blifs will

not

not prevail.—But his Lordſhip could only advert to the adult and married part of the ſex, who, being in every ſenſe *Femmes Couvertes*, would certainly prefer being *properly covered*, in a *manly way*, to the *toyiſh rigs and wriggles* of *Boarding-School Sports*, and *girliſh Paſtimes*.

According to his Lordſhip's Bill, the parties divorced cannot marry again to each other, or to any one, till the expiration of a twelvemonth. This puts us in mind of the laws and cuſtoms amongſt the Turks with reſpect to Marriages and Divorces. " The opu-
" lent have often three or four wives,
" and perhaps as many concubines ; but
" if they chuſe to abide by the more
" laudable part of the law, and keep
" only to wives, it is equally conve-
" nient, for they may change and

" change

" change as often as the number will
" admit —After divorce, they may re
" take the fame woman a fecond, but
" not a third time, unlefs fhe has been
" married to another hufband. No man
" can marry a divorced woman fooner
" than four months and a half after a
" total feparation from the former huf-
" band. The man may oblige the di-
" vorced woman to keep a child till it
" is two years old*."

Having faid thus much concerning
Divorces, the Reader may not be difpleafed to be acquainted with the nature
and ceremonial of marriage amongft the
Turks, from the fame author.

" The Turks are conveniently cir-
" cumftanced in regard to the matri-

---

* Vide Obfervations on the Laws, Manners,
and Cuftoms of the Turks. Vol. II. p 85.

" monial

" monial tie. The Grand Seignior is
" entirely exempt from it, he claims
" the privilege Mahomet reserved for
" himself, and to avoid a formal con-
" tract of affinity, or, in the Turkish
" phrafe, not to mix blood with any
" family in his empire, he has no wife,
" but only concubines. The first who
" brings him a fon is called the *Sultana*
" *Hafeki* She is crowned with flowers,
" takes on her the prerogatives of a
" wife, and governs the Haram.

" OTHER Turks are allowed four
" wives. They may marry, as it is
" called, *Kaibin*, that is, they appear
' before the tribunal of juftice, declare
" the woman to be their wife, and enter
" into an obligation, that whenever they
" fhall think proper to difmifs her, they
" will maintain the children, and give
" her a certain ftipulated fum, which

" they

" they proportion either to their cir-
" cumſtances, or to the time they judge
" it may be convenient for them to co-
" habit with her. It is no ſtain to a
" woman's character that ſhe is thus
' put away, nor much impediment to
" her finding another huſband * "

We find alſo that the girls, in order
that they may not be deceived by a
rumbling huſband, have a cuſtom,
ſomewhat like *Bundling*, in *Wales* and
New England, for though they do not
bed with their intended huſbands, they
inſiſt upon taking a view of their propoſed mate in *puris naturalibus*, from a
convenient concealment, without being
put to the bluſh at ſuch an exhibition.
If they approve of this candidate for
matrimony, they readily conſent to give

---

* Vide Obſervations on the Laws, Manners,
and Cuſtoms of the Turks, Vol II. p 84.

him their hands, but if he should not answer their expectations, and his virility should seem doubtful, they are allowed to reject him, without assigning any reason. Such a custom introduced into *England* would be of great benefit to the Ladies, and might be a means of preventing Divorces, as the Ladies of rank and fashion could make this inspection with impunity, and without having their modesty called in question. Many a V—NE and P—Y could then have no just reason to complain, or be able to apologize, on account of their husbands defects, for their infidelities to the marriage bed.

CHAP.

C H A P. XXXVIII.

An Introduction at Madame Le P——'s.
A little Coup de Charlatanerie *in Intrigue, which had nearly proved fatal to this Lady. An uncommon Imposture, and a ridiculous Discovery. The means taken by Madame* Le P—— *to restore the Dignity and Reputation of her House. Some Account of the* Amourettes, Hoydens, *and* Graces. *Impositions of Lottery Office-Keepers,* Jews *and* Refiners.

WE had like to have forgot waiting upon our old friend and acquaintance Madame *Le P——*, in *South Molton-Street*; but *though last not least in Love.* This Lady has the honour of entertaining the first nobility in England,

land, as well as the Foreign Miniſters, in
as elegant a ſtile as any Lady Abbeſs in
the purlieus of St *James's*. An unlucky diſcovery that was lately made by
Count H—o, had brought this Seminary into ſome little diſrepute. She had
wrote to the Count, and informed him,
that ſhe was that evening to be viſited
by a young Lady, who had juſt eloped
from her Relations, who were of a noble family; but that being croſſed in
love, and her admirer having wedded
another young Lady of her acquaintance, ſhe was reſolved that night to
ſacrifice herſelf to the Paphian Goddeſs,
as that was her appointed nuptial night,
and her rival was married that day.
The Count, who is always very gallant
upon theſe occaſions, ard never lets an
opportunity ſlip of being introduced to
a fine woman, eſpecially if ſhe is upon
the footing of a modeſt lady, attended

M 4 the

the fummons at the hour appointed, and was introduced to Mifs Lar—che: this was the temporary name, at leaft, fhe bore. Mifs L—e had received a very genteel education, and had in her red veftal days kept fome of the beft company. accordingly, fhe was very capable of receiving the Count in a manner fuitable to his moft fanguine expectations. Being acquainted with many of the firft families in *England*, fhe could fpeak with much propriety upon their alliances and connexions; which, added to her being a pretty good Miftrefs of French, and having alfo a tolerably harmonious voice, which was improved by her having learnt mufic, the Count was eafily perfuaded that Mifs Lar—che was precifely fuch a perfon as Madame Le P—— had reprefented. In this prefumption

he

he enjoyed her company with great satisfaction; and having prepared himself by meretricious arts, was inclined to believe he was as vigorous as ever, and had actually possessed a pure Vestal. Upon his retiring, he made a very handsome present, and promised to renew his visit in a few days.

HOWEVER, in the interim, falling in company with Monsieur M— P—N the R——— Minister, he was boasting of this lucky adventure, and saying, that he was very well pleased to find that his athletic power had not subsided, for that he had actually got a *Pucelage* the very night before. Monsieur M— P—N, said, he was not at all surprized at the Count's abilities; but upon a description of the young Lady in question, it so exactly tallied with the resemblance of one he had himself enjoyed a few

M 5   nights

nights before in *King's-Place*, under the name of REY—LDS, that he offered to wager the Count twenty guineas, that if he sent for her to the *Bedford Arms* under the latter name, she would make her appearance there in consequence of his card.

THE wager was laid, and Miss R—Y—N—LDS sent for that very night to the *Bedford Arms*. The Count was placed in an adjacent room, and through a peep-hole made on purpose, could view the Lady. In less than an hour the porter returned with Miss R———DS in a chair. The Count was planted as agreed upon, the Lady introduced, and he was soon convinced that she was the identical female who had been introduced to him, as the eloped Miss LAR—CHE, at Madame Le P—'s.

THIS

THIS difcovery gieatly enraged the Count, not fo much at being impofed upon by Madame LE P——, as, in confequence of having vaunted his good fortune in intrigve, he was obliged to ftand the raillery of the whole Diplomatic Body the next time they dined together, which was a few days after, when he was complimented on all hands for his great good fortune with the Ladies, and 'for his uncommon athletic poweis of getting maidenheads with the facility and vigoui of a young fellow of twenty.

THIS unluc'.y difcovery was for a time veiy pernicious to Mad. LE P—— and her Seminary, as fhe thereby loft, foi a while, the cuftom of all the Foreign Minifters; and this ftory being circulated, many of her other male vifitors often fufpected her veracity upon fimilai occafions.

HOWEVER, Mad. LE P—— having found it expedient to recruit her Nunnery from the beſt and moſt original reſources, ſhe ſoon recovered moſt of her cuſtomers ; as, to ſpeak in vulgar phraſeology, her's was now *one of the beſt Fleſh-Markets in town.*

IN leſs than a month ſhe had ſelected two very pretty Pariſians, juſt arrived from *France*, and who were quite new faces in *London* They were ſiſters, and went by the name of *Meſdemoiſelles Amourette:* indeed they were very well entitled to this name ; for Lord C—LE, upon being firſt introduced to them to take his choice, ſaid to them, " *Ma foy, mes* " *Dames, vous êtes jolis comme les Amours* " *mêmes!—Il n'y a pas mien de choiſir, il* " *faut vous prendre tour à tour.*" Beſides her lovely Pariſians, ſhe had a very comely cargo of *Engliſh* Hoydens, freſh

as

as the morn, and arrived in the laft *York* waggon. BETTY WILL—s, LUCY CLEVL—D, JENNY PR—-TT, NANCY P—RSONS, (not the celebrated NANCY P—RSONS) were all fine, wholefome wenches, who had indeed been deluded into this kind of fervitude, inftead of that of *all-work*, for which they made this journey to *London*. Befides thefe Inmates, fhe was frequently vifited by the three Graces, whom we have already introduced in the characters of Mifs CARTER, Mifs ARMSTR—G, and Mifs STANLEY.

THUS did Madame LE P— not only reftore the reputation of her houfe, but recalled the moft valuable of the *Corps Diplomatique*, who were vaftly enraptured with the vivacity, as well as beauty of the *Amourettes*, and could occafion-

ally,

ally, for the fake of variety, revel with
the Hoydens, and fometimes the Graces.
Thus, by blending together Parifian
frivolity with country rufticity and
courtly grace, they united almoft every
diftinct point of Beauty into one focus,
and might be faid to have as complete
and variegated a Seraglio as the Grand
Seignior himfelf.

WE cannot refrain mentioning here
two whimfical, and in fome degree mortifying adventures, that happened to
the *Amourettes* foon after their arrival
here   Thinking it a certainty of making their fortunes in the Metropolis of
England, which was the Emporium of
wealth, as well as vice and folly, they
judged it expedient to purfue every
avenue to the Temple of the Blind
Goddefs that prefented itfelf to their
view, and accordingly the Lottery
feemed

feemed to them a certain routine to *twenty thoufand* pounds, by a mere *coup-de main*. This being the time of draw-ing, they failed not every night infur-ing to the utmoft extent of their pockets, and the firft week drained them of up-wards of forty pounds. The fecond week wore a more aufpicious afpect. but the event proved otherwife. The firft day they had apparently a run of good luck, and when they had infured upwards of ten pounds, and were in expectation of receiving more than two hundred—that very night the Lottery - Office, where they had depofited their money, fhut up, and the Office-keeper decamped *à la four-cine*. The next day they were equally unfortunate, as an Office-keeper refufed to pay, under pretence that there was fome fraud in the infurance of a parti-cular number, it having been done for confiderable fums at all the Lottery-

offices

offices in town. Thus impofed upon, they found themfelves, at the end of the drawing, near two hundred pounds out of pocket, though, if they had been paid according to their juft demands, they would have cleared, at leaft, fifteen hundred pounds.

ANOTHER accident they met with was alfo very mortifying, though not fo effentially interefting. Two Jew Brokers ufed often to vifit them, and they conftantly made their compliments in light gold, but they had received their cue from Madame Le P———, never to think of weighing money, that they might not affront her cuftomers: they made no remonftrances, therefore, to their Benefactors, but conftantly difpofed of the light gold at a refiner's, to a confiderable lofs, as will appear by the fequel. In the courfe of one week they

were

were obliged to fell thirty light guineas, at the lofs of two fhillings upon each guinea · and fo much do fome of the gentlemen-*refiners refine* upon honefty, that every one of the guineas the *Amourettes* received in exchange, were lighter than thofe difpofed of, and before they could get a paffable guinea for either of their original ones, they were four fhillings and fixpence out of pocket.--- This was paying poundage with a vengeance; and when, in jocularity, they informed their Levitic friends of the event, one of them replied, " G---d's " nounds, me would have tooken every " one of them backs, at only tree fchil- " ings defcount."

CHAP.

CHAP XXXIX.

The present Situation and Pursuits of the principal Dramatis Personæ brought upon the Stage of the NOCTURNAL REVELS, and being the last Chapter, concludes with the Moral, which must appear obvious to every Reader.

HAVING given a variety of pictures of Keepers, Petticoat-Pensioners, Old Virgins, Wives and Widows, troubled with the *furor uterinus*, Young Letchers debilitated, and impotent old Dotards flattered into a belief of their vigour and amorous abilities, the Portraits of the most celebrated Thais's and Demi-reps upon the *Ton*, in a variety of whimsical, lascivious and meretricious devices, we now approach the period of taking leave of these

Worthy

Worthy Characters, after having taken a review of their present situation and future pursuits.

Mrs Goadby's Nunnery is still in great esteem in *Marlborough-Street*, and she proposes laying in a fresh stock of clean goods, warranted proof, for the Races and Watering-places, during the ensuing Summer.

Mrs. Adáms, Mis. Dubery, Mrs. Pendergast, Mrs. Windsor and Mrs. Matthews, still preserve the dignity of their houses, and the immaculate reputation of *King's-Place*.

Mrs Nels—n is *Semper-e-adem*; but not, according to the Irish translation, *Worse and Worse*, for that would be *impossible!*

Nilly

NELLY ELL——T is grown fo very fat and unwieldy, that fhe is obliged to ftudy Aretin in all his poftures, to render herfelf acceffible to little S——T, who is fo fmall, that he can fcarce penetrate her *porte cochere*, even with the affiftance of Gale's elaftic bedfteads, now fo greatly in vogue. However, NELLY having lately made a felect fett of acquaintance with fome of the firft-rate kept women, fhe carries on a very pretty flourifhing trade, in fupplying the deficiences of their fumbling Keepers, who fupport them entirely for the honour of being thought men of Gallantry.

MRS. W——STON ftill poffeffes the good opinion of her noble and polite cuftomers, and particularly the favour and protection of Lord GRO——R.

MRS.

Mrs. Bradsh—w continues to entertain her noble friends according to the most polished Etiquette, assisted by Miss Ken—dy, Mrs. Armst—d, and several other Ladies of equal eminence, upon the list of *Demireps* of the Haut Ton.

Miss N—lson has got the *Tea-pot* into her *wake*, after having failed in obeying the first signal, this Frigate having put into the wrong port through mistake.

Lady Lig——r, after an elopement of about a dozen weeks, judged it prudential (her purse being entirely exhausted) to seek another remedy, besides that which had been salutary for the recovery of her health, for the repletion of her pocket—to return to her old friend L.—ke in Yorkshire.

THE *Bird of Paradise* ftill continues to keep up her connexion with her generous keeper TU—N—R, who overlooks the peccadilloes of her conduct, and has even forgiven her appearance at Mrs PENDERGAST's *Bal d'Amour.*

THE lovely EMILY was upon the point of being taken into keeping, by a gentleman who had juft been appointed to a confiderable employment under Adminiftration, and the emoluments of whofe office could very well enable him to fupport her in luxury and grandeur.

KITTY FRED——K we have already fixed with a falary of a hundred a-year, and board-wages of ten guineas a week, in the *New-Buildings.*

THE

The Graces, C—rt—r, Arm-st—ng and Stanl—y, flourish away, as usual, with taste and elegance, resolving not to tie themselves to any one man, but to rove at large, where pleasure or profit leads the way.

Lady Ad——ms having seen much service, is somewhat weather-beaten, having been in many a storm, tossed about upon rocks and shoals, and this winter narrowly escaped foundering upon a lee-shore in *Tavistock-Row, Covent-Garden*. The last time George S—lw—n saw her, he swore from these circumstances, that Lady Ad——ms was to all intents and purposes a misnomer, and that he should hereafter call her *Old Mother Eve*.

Lady G——r is very bountiful of her favours. T—rn—r would be her

favourite

favourite man, did not his avarice compel her to fly to the arms of Sir G——
T—— P——, and others, whose purse-
strings are more easily dilated. This
assertion is supported by the Author of
The *Torpedo* :

" Sated at length with Ca-lm nd-l-y's charms,
" Gr--ven r takes T-rn-r to her arms,
  " That avaricious Prig
" Such is the vigorous Damsel's zeal,
" She tries each species of the Eel,
  " From Conger down to Grig."

In the Note to Grig we are told—
" A small species of Eel, by which ap-
" pellation Sir G— T— P— was dis-
" tinguished in his youth; not from
" his vivacity, but from its similitude
" to the abbreviation of his own name "

Clara Hayw—d figures off and on
the Stage, in various parts and attitudes,

tudes, and generally meets with applaufe, particularly in her under parts.

MRS BRAD——Y fticks *en Morpton*,
as if cemented, to her long Trowel and
the Macaroni Bricklayer.

LUCY WILL—MS has got a pretty
running trade, and often entertains Earl
P—Y with a fentimental dialogue, for
which he pays very handfomely; and
fometimes, in the full vigour of youth,
he makes an impotent attempt upon her
latent charms.

EMILY C—LH—ST is ftill in the purlieus of *King's-Place*, occafionally at one
or other Nunnery, as bufinefs requires.

THE lucky and critical efcapes of Mifs
P—R and Mifs M—C have warned
thefe young Ladies to be upon their guard

against the artful seductions of then own sex, as well as the treachery of ours. The first of these young Ladies is upon the point of being married to a gentleman of considerable rank and fortune: The latter receives the addresses of a young Nobleman, who, it is believed, will, as soon as he comes of age, offer her his hand in an honourable way.

The Stable-yard Messalina we left two Chapters ago in a salacious situation, in which she has remained ever since, and the General, it is said, is much indisposed, from the effects of the provocatives which he took to enable him to gratify the full extent of her desires.

The other Ladies whom we have introduced in this Historical Drama remain in *statu quo*, with very little variation,

tion, except in their faces, which in a morning, before the application of the cosmetic art, so far from inviting to amorous dalliance, rather create disgust, but about noon, by the assistance of BAILEY and WARREN, those great and eminent manufacturers of female charms, become as enchanting as ever

As to our Male *Dramatis Personæ*, they still pursue nearly the same career as they have done for some years Lord FUMBLE repaired regularly, as long as he could crawl, four times a-week to Mrs. PENDERGAST's, to indulge his whims and caprices with a brace of new faces. But he is to that Lady's great affliction—now no more! Lord PYEBALD is ever upon the hunt after a tid-bit, which he cannot enjoy; and in this pursuit he prances about the *New-Buildings*, in his shabby great coat, and still more shab-

by

by hat, but with a fword, to de-
rote the Gentleman. Count H——G
full has a ftrong hankering after women
of family and breeding; but takes care
not to be fo grofsly impofed upon as he
was by Madame Le P——. The other
Members of the Diplomatic Body purfue their old career of vifiting the Nunneries, after they have made up their
difpatches. Unfortunately for poor
W——LK——NSON, the Swedifh Ambaffador made a difagreeable difcovery the
other evening at Mrs. DUBERY's, fhe being introduced as a Nun, in the ordinary
routine, when he judged fhe was waiting
for him at home, chafte as Penelope.
The confequence was, he immediately
broke off his connexion with her, and
fhe is now obliged to ply in *King's-Place*,
from abfolute neceffity; whereas, before
this accident, fhe only made her appearance there through mere wantonnefs, as
Mrs.

Mrs. WOFFINGTON faid fhe went to *Bath*.

MONSIEUR M—N P—N, the Ruffian Minifter, is now in treaty with an Opera-Dancer, who has cut a caper into his heart, and made him forget all the Nuns of *King's-Place*. Signora Z—LLI modeftly demands only twenty guineas a-week, with a carriage, and new liveries for her fervants. Whether the Minifter will comply with her requeft, is a matter of doubt,—in the mean while fhe flaunts away with her *Cicifbeo*, and thinks fhe has made a certain conqueft of this Member of the Diplomatic Body. It is, however, faid, that he has changed the direction of his amorous battery, and planted his falacious artillery againft the pretty ideot, Mrs BAD-D—LY; but there are fome reafons to think, that her *covered way* muft either

ther be taken by *storm*, or *blown up*, as we are well affured, the *port* itfelf is fo *undermined*, and the *combuftibles* fo violent, as to admit of no affailant, whilft FIREBRAND TONY, chief Engineer, has the infpection of the Works.

HAVING thus difpofed of the moft material of our *Dramatis Perfonæ*, we fhall take leave of the Reader, and conclude this Volume with a tranflation of our Motto, for the information of the mere Englifh Reader.

" I LOOK upon it as my mafter-piece,
" that I have found out how a young
" fellow may know the difpofition and
" behaviour of Harlots; and by early
" knowing, come to detect them."

F I N I S.

Lately Published,

I.

In Two Parts   Price 3s. 6d.

THE DIABOLIAD   A POEM. Dedicated
to the WORST MAN in his MAJESTY's
DOMINIONS.

II.

Price 1s. 6d.

The DIABO-LADY   Or, A MATCH in
HELL   A POEM. Dedicated to the WORST
WOMAN in his MAJESTY's DOMINIONS.

A New Edition, with large Additions

O faireft of Creation, laft and beft
Of all God's Works, creature in whom excelled
Whatever can to fight or thought be formed,
Holy, divine, good, amiable, or fweet!
How art thou loft!   MILTON.

III.

Price 2s. 6d.

The FIRST OF APRIL   Or, The
TRIUMPHS of FOLLY. A POEM   Dedicated to a CELEBRATED DUCHESS

By the AUTHOR of The DIABOLIAD.

A NEW EDITION

——Doft thou call me Fool, Boy——
All thy other Titles thou haft given away
That thou waft born with!   SHAKESPEARE.

IV.

Price 1s. 6d.

The TORPEDO, A POEM to the ELECTRICAL EEL.

Addressed to Mr. JOHN HUNTER, Surgeon:

And Dedicated to the

Right Honourable LORD CHOLMONDELEY.

The Fourth Edition, with large Additions

" Electricity will probably soon be considered as the great vivifying principle of Nature, by which she carries on most of her operations.

"——Some years ago a Lady of Switzerland was strangely affected by it."

BRYDONE'S TRAVELS.

V

Price 1s. 6d.

MIMOSA Or, The SENSITIVE PLANT. A POEM.

Dedicated to Mr. BANKS

And Addressed to KITT FREDERICK.
Duchess of QUEENSBURY, Elect

————————I started back,
It started back but pleased I soon returned;
Pleas'd, it return'd as soon, with answering looks
Of sympathy and love.

MILTON.